FROM THE
GROUND UP

FROM THE

GROUND UP

Horsemanship

for the Adult Rider

BRENDA IMUS

HOWELL BOOK HOUSE
New York

MAXWELL MACMILLAN CANADA
Toronto

MAXWELL MACMILLAN INTERNATIONAL
New York   Oxford   Singapore   Sydney

This book is not intended as a substitute for personal instruction in horsemanship by professional instructors. Neither the Publisher nor the Author shall be responsible for any injuries incurred by following the instructions given in this book.

Copyright © 1992 by Brenda Imus

Howell Book House Maxwell Macmillan Canada, Inc.
Macmillan Publishing Company 1200 Eglinton Avenue East
866 Third Avenue Suite 200
New York, NY 10022 Don Mills, Ontario M3C 3N1

Macmillan Publishing Company is part of the Maxwell Communication Group of Companies.

Library of Congress Cataloging-in-Publication Data
Imus, Brenda.
  From the ground up : horsemanship for the adult rider / Brenda Imus.
    p.   cm.
  Includes bibliographical references and index.
  ISBN 0-87605-830-6
  1. Horsemanship. I. Title.
SF309.I47   1992
798.2—dc20   91-26301
                                                                        CIP

Macmillan books are available at special discounts for bulk purchases for sales promotions, premiums, fund-raising, or educational use. For details, contact:

  Special Sales Director
  Macmillan Publishing Company
  866 Third Avenue
  New York, NY 10022

10 9 8 7 6 5 4 3 2 1

Printed in the United States of America

*This book
is lovingly dedicated to*
CHAMP,
my first, and best, teacher.

Contents

Acknowledgments

This work has come about largely as a result of the help, expertise and encouragement of a number of people. I want to thank Kathleen Cronk of Butternut Brook Equine Center for her able photographic assistance and excellent suggestions, and for her unstinting patience and cheerfulness. Jon Elder of Jon Elder Productions took time from a hectic schedule to provide the darkroom work for the photographs. Brita Barlow contributed her time and considerable artistic talents to produce most of the line drawings. I'm indebted to the folks at Stagecoach West, who allowed me to tear their store apart so I could get clear shots of saddles and such. R. P. ("Doc") Draudt, D.V.M., is a good friend and valued resource who helped ensure the accuracy of the health care chapter.

I am grateful also to Coleen Carlson, for helping to see me through what is perhaps the most difficult trial a horse lover ever faces: losing a very special horse.

Thanks especially to Hugh, my husband, encourager and best friend always.

Foreword

I don't know Brenda Imus personally; we've never met. But I have read hundreds—maybe even thousands—of pages of her writings on horses and horsemen. Over the years, she has been a frequent contributor to *Horse and Horseman* magazine . . . and out of that long-distance relationship, I've learned that, while I may not know Brenda Imus, I'm sure we know a lot of the same horses!

Brenda Imus describes love of the horse as a condition that borders on mania with some; an instinctive longing, perhaps, for more simple times and earth-bound ideals. Because she understands it and shares in this compulsion, Brenda has given novice riders of all ages a comprehensive guide to horsemanship that is written with love.

The title of her book, *From the Ground Up*, constitutes a promise, and I think it is safe to say the triumph promised is inclusive of both horse and rider. In what can only be considered an unusual twist, Brenda's training methods begin with getting to know your horse—and end with getting to know yourself. Discovering training practices and techniques of discipline—including self-discipline—with which you are comfortable is half the struggle for any new rider.

Communication between humans can be strained—not to mention exhausting and infuriating, at times—but, at least, such an exchange is possible. Communication with horses is more a guesswork affair. They can't speak, so the clues must take a more subtle form. Brenda Imus gives the horse owner or new rider confidence. The pages in this book can and should serve as a constant source of information and confirmation. From my observation, virtually all horse-related problems can be solved by a quick thumb-through of this book.

Other books have dealt with the technical aspects of horseownership in a plodding, step-by-step manner. Those tomes have explored tack and grooming with a thoroughness that can only be described as boring, if not downright painful. Rather than fall into that trap, Brenda Imus provides an overview of important equine concerns. All the basics still are covered, but in the author's somewhat unorthodox style. Among other things, she has a full appreciation of the reader's intelligence and doesn't insult it. Brenda's goal is to make the rider comfortable with the horse. The quickest path to this hard-sought but beneficial partnership between man and animal is always lined with knowledge. The author is not one to romanticize the responsibilities of horse ownership. She makes it totally clear that this is one possession that requires a great deal more than just desire. As she puts it, "The heart and body must be in sync."

The book itself makes excellent reading for those prepurchase days. I certainly would recommend that anyone planning on buying that first horse read this book from cover to cover. After the sale has been completed and there is a need for practical, day-to-day work, care and training of the horse, it probably is too late for the first-time owner to have a change of mind. A careful reading of *From the Ground Up* should afford the potential buyer a clear preview of what can be expected in the post-purchase days. It's not all riding off into the sunset, folks.

This volume also would make an excellent gift for anyone thinking of buying a first horse and probably should be required reading for the novice. If nothing else, Brenda Imus wants her readers to take stock of their own sincerity. In short, her message is: You don't have to own a horse to appreciate one.

In our media-laden age, preparing for life's responsibilities has never been easier! That, at least, is what some would have us think. There are books detailing the stages of childbirth, the difficulties of marriage and the pain of loss. Less pivotal events, those that add to the quality of our lives, also are explored by the media in no small way. Brenda Imus has taken advantage of the fact that today's consumer has learned to anticipate these experiences. Thus, *From the Ground Up* allows each reader a knowledgeable insight into the day-to-day world of the horse owner. Stripping through the layers of awe experienced by so many, the author allows a love of horses to flourish on a foundation of truth—not a cloud of dreams.

Brenda Imus writes with a skill born of her own love for horses. Her words reflect patience, honesty and humor. She would be the ideal next-door neighbor for a new horse owner. Her book is for those who can't just pick up and move next door.

Jack Lewis, Editor
Horse and Horseman
Capistrano Beach, California

Introduction

When beginning a project such as this, the temptation is to start at point A, proceed to point B and then continue on in orderly fashion to point Z, or "The End."

But writing about horsemanship is another matter. It is a discipline that cannot, in the truest sense, be taught, for horsemanship is a spiritual affair. A genuine understanding of horses begins in the heart, and only incidentally is worked out using practical methods in the everyday world.

With the exception of certain Amish or other sectarian communities, horses are a living anachronism—their presence has become unjustified in our modern world. We no longer use them to help fight our wars or to transport us, and less and less to herd our cattle or work our fields. Besides this, they are expensive to purchase and keep, they are often difficult to deal with and they require vast amounts of time in a world that places a premium on every minute.

Nevertheless, there are people for whom the desire to associate with horses is a compulsion bordering on mania, or so some nonequestrians might think. For those of us who got a late start in equestrian life, this is especially true.

The usual drawbacks to becoming involved in horse activities are multiplied seven times over in the lives of those of us who claim adult responsibility. There are likely to be excessive demands upon our time and financial resources. With the years come increased poundage, decreased physical strength and agility and a growing desire to avoid bodily harm.

Yet within some of us is a cry as old as the human race. Though we may muffle this disquieting cry, it will not be silenced or placated. No matter how successful or happy or accomplished we become in any other area of life, our hearts continue to sound the childish plea: "I want a horse!"

This book is written for those who have heeded, plan to heed or can be induced to heed, that plea. It is written for the novice horseman. While many people can dance, write or draw a picture, few are truly dancers, poets or artists. The ability to handle horses does not mean that one is a horseman. Horsemanship is a state of mind and heart, regardless of practical skill—though knowledge and skill add immeasurably to our enjoyment of horses. The goal of this book is to help you gain enough knowledge, confidence, good judgment and practical skill to enable you to thoroughly enjoy your association with the horse.

Novice adult horsemen, whether twenty or seventy years of age, whether male or female, have unique needs. You need the basics of horse psychology and handling methods clearly explained, without condescension. You need to recognize and learn the best ways to deal with your various limitations. After getting off to a late start, you want to learn as quickly, but as safely, as possible. Because most horsemen eventually encounter problems of one sort or another, you need to be offered straightforward, safe and practical ways to handle them. You need to learn to trust your instincts. You also need to be told when it's wise not to attempt something yourself but to seek professional help. All of which this book will attempt to do.

There are many excellent books that teach the basics of health care and how to evaluate conformation. I won't do here what has already been handled so well elsewhere. I give only the briefest overview of these subjects and share with you my own sometimes unorthodox views. I encourage you to browse the tack shops and bookstores, consult the Recommended Reading, and deepen your understanding of these important elements of horsemanship.

But, for now, let's get on with matters of the hand and heart.

One

THE CHARACTER
OF THE HORSE

Of all the animals on earth, there are few to rival the horse for the number of myths, folktales and "expert opinions" regarding its basic character. Some would have us believe the horse is one of God's more foolish creatures, with a brain capacity little higher than that of an earthworm and no more innate reliability—aside from the effects of harsh discipline—than Alice's Mad Hatter. Others attribute to the horse supernatural powers bordering on those of mythical or angelic beings.

Few people adhere long to the first opinion, for familiarity with the horse breeds respect—sometimes awe. Even as I write, I'm looking out my study window to the pasture where my Palomino gelding is pastured. Yesterday we sent his pasture mate, a mare, out to be bred. So today he's especially lonely and griefstricken. I'm sitting two stories high, several hundred feet away, behind a sun-glazed window. With no obvious way of knowing that I've looked up from my work—or even that I'm still on the same planet he inhabits—he raises his head, peers intently in my direction and nickers softly. I meet his eye. After a moment, he goes quietly back to grazing. I cannot explain this kind of phenomenon. I only know that a special bond exists between some horses and some people.

On the other hand, it is a grave mistake to overly romanticize the horse. We're considering a 1,000-plus pound, flesh-and-bone, sometimes unpredictable animal that will prove to be a dangerous pet unless discipline and respect for human beings are firmly instilled.

There is no end of contradictions in the horse's character. Most foals are born with an essentially skittish, shy nature. Nevertheless, a horse may grow to become magnificently daring and bold, or terribly aggressive and dangerous. Innately wary of the unusual and unexpected, he can be trained to march proudly in parades, fight in battle and help mounted police create order out of chaos. By nature a lazy grazing animal, he can be induced to work—and work hard—for hours and days on end. Instinctively fearful of predators and pools of water, and dependent upon keeping all four feet on the ground as a primary defense, the horse can be induced to carry lions, tigers and bears on his back during a circus performance and to leap six-foot-high walls into an unfathomed pool of water, merely at his master's bidding.

All this shows that the horse is remarkable in his ability to adapt to humans—as long as those involved in his training and use are sensitive to his basic needs and individual characteristics.

EVERY HORSE IS UNIQUE

While every horse is born with certain qualities common to all—curiosity and a seemingly insatiable appetite, for example—each possesses a unique temperament, personality and athletic ability. Not all horses are suited to all purposes. Nor can anyone expect to get along with every horse that comes along, any more than one can expect to get along with every person in the world. A naturally "hot," high-spirited horse might be appropriate as a barrel-racer's mount but make a poor pleasure horse. Another, while bred for the track, may not be successful at racing, yet go on to become a brilliant dressage performer. An extremely unathletic, slow mount might be just right for a timid, unathletic child. A mentally tough horse that is insensitive to his rider's aids would probably get along fine with a heavy-handed rider, while a more sensitive animal could be ruined in the same hands.

A HANDLER'S RESPONSIBILITIES

A horse's lifelong character as a service animal is shaped and molded through his experience with handlers. It is therefore the handler's responsibility to determine where a horse's talents lie and bring him along accordingly—or pass the animal on to someone more likely to do so. Sympathetic handlers, attuned to the horse's basic needs and individual qualities, almost always produce good, reliable riding mounts. Ignorant, insensitive handling invariably produces disaster.

For this reason, stories abound in the horse world of animals that were considered good for little more than the slaughter house but with sensitive and carefully considered handling, became outstanding in their discipline.

A thirty-two-year-old Morgan mare is currently the country's premiere riding horse for people who are severely physically handicapped. At two years of age, this horse was so rebellious that her owners sold her as a bronc on the rodeo circuit. Through good luck and circumstance, she was eventually purchased by people who understood her talents and eccentricities, and brought her along accordingly. She was trained not only to go quietly under saddle, but also to be aware of the special needs of her riders. She has enriched the lives of hundreds of people who might not otherwise have ever known the freedom and independence of sitting a fine, reliable horse.

And then there's John Henry, the remarkable Thoroughbred race horse that was considered so unruly and physically unpromising that as a two-year-old he was gelded and sold for less than two thousand dollars to a horse dealer. Several people bought and sold John Henry, until finally he was purchased by a man who hired a trainer who came to understand (a) that this horse needed to be raced on turf rather than dirt and (b) in order to get a good performance out of John Henry, his handlers needed to throw away the rule books on how to train and ride stakes horses and just let him have his own way. John Henry went on to make racing history by becoming the nation's top-winning turf racer and by having a long racing career many years beyond what is usual for a Thoroughbred race horse.

An example from closer to home: I once acquired a lovely seven-year-old Appaloosa mare with a bad reputation. Her former owner—a heavy-handed rider—claimed this mare was a "plain rank horse" and traded her to a dealer friend of mine for a tough old gelding. Fortunately, my friend realized that this horse, despite her problems, was basically a kind, ultrasensitive animal that suffered mainly from inappropriate handling. She thought the mare would make a good mount for me because she lacked the quickness that a younger, more agile rider might want but was nevertheless a smooth, long-strided animal that would get me down the rail or the trail in comfort and style. She also had the temperament of a pet, which is a quality I like.

It so happened that I had a Quarter Horse gelding in my barn that I'd come to dislike. He was standoffish and extremely unpredictable, and sometimes exhibited a mean streak, especially around other horses. Since ours is a small barn, my chances of reforming him by exposing him to other animals that could put him in his place were minimal.

On the other hand, my dealer friend runs a stable and horse-breeding operation, and has horses by the barnful. So I traded my Quarter Horse gelding for the Appaloosa mare.

Although the mare, Love (a barn name she acquired within the first few days of coming home), did need some work, I didn't find her at all difficult. We seemed to understand one another in a way the Quarter Horse gelding and I never had. I spent just a few weeks working with her before taking her on a county-wide, organized trail ride. She behaved impeccably. Another rider who knew her in her former life could hardly believe this was the same mare that had been such a renegade. Our family likes this horse so much that we've sent her out to be bred; we'd like another horse with a few of her fine qualities. My daughter plans to use her for 4-H shows, and I have no reservations whatever about her doing this. Love has become a reliable using horse.

But that's not the end of the story. Remember the tough old gelding my friend gave the rider in exchange for the Appy? The last I heard, that horse and rider were getting along very well. And the unpredictable Quarter Horse gelding I traded for Love? He got sent to pasture with several different groups of horses, until he learned he wasn't so tough after all. Today he's a reliable working horse in a stable string. There he's not expected to be a pet, and that suits him fine.

The secret to the success of all three horses was my dealer friend, who correctly sized up the character of each horse and each person, and made appropriate matches. She has earned the title of horsewoman.

The trick to bringing out the best in a horse lies in learning how to read and respond to different horses. While most people can eventually learn how to get along with a single horse, a true horseman has the desire to understand and know more about all horses in order to be able to work comfortably with different horses. While some people are born with more innate horse sense than others, it is a skill that can be—and to some extent, must be—learned. The only way to learn is to practice.

And the only way to practice is to be around horses. Lots and lots of horses.

Two
GETTING STARTED

You want to get into horses? Great! But don't buy a horse of your own. At least, not yet.

As we've seen, the main difference between a novice horseman and an accomplished one is that the latter has learned through study and experience how to read and respond to horses. This process takes time, and the amount of time it takes depends on how much opportunity the learner has—or makes—to watch and work with different horses.

Purchasing a horse limits you to working with one horse at a time when you most need experience with a variety of horses. Also, by working with many kinds of horses, you will lessen the possibility of purchasing a spoiled, unsound or otherwise inappropriate animal when the time comes for you to purchase. You will have made an informed decision about the kind of horse you want and will have learned who to trust to help you find it. Expanding your equine horizons helps put you in the way of more and better horse-purchasing deals. After a short time, you should have learned a few tricks of the horse-dealing trade yourself. This is an essential element of your education—there are plenty of sharks who masquerade as friendly, honest horse dealers.

So where to start, if not with your own horse? The logical first step is to invest in riding lessons. Take them as often as possible, at least weekly.

INSTRUCTION AND CHOOSING A STYLE

While cost is certainly one criterion you need to take into consideration when looking for an appropriate riding instructor, it should not be the deciding factor. Arrange to have your first several lessons at different stables until you find an instructor, price structure, and riding style you're comfortable with. This will enable you to ride different horses and to try different riding styles: hunt seat, Western stock, saddle seat, dressage, etc. Most riding establishments offer lessons in all or most of these categories but specialize in just one or two. Go with the establishment's specialty, and don't be afraid to try one of those "postage stamp"-size English saddles. The feel you get for the horse in some of these saddles is unparalleled—although Western close-contact saddles are getting better all the time and may offer the extra feeling of security some riders need. Experiment to find out what you like.

SELECTING AN INSTRUCTOR

A few things to look for in a riding establishment: Be sure your instructor takes time to actually teach you, so you aren't just stuck up on top of a horse and told to ride around a pasture or an arena for an hour. The

A good riding instruction facility will provide a sensible, sound schooling horse and a controlled riding environment.

horses should look well groomed and in good condition; they should breathe easily and not limp at any gait. If a horse you are riding evidences physical distress, insist on ending the lesson. If the instructor is not sympathetic to the horse's needs, don't return to that establishment. Lesson horses should be willing, well mannered and reasonably responsive to their riders. They must never offer to bite, kick, buck, rear or bolt. The establishment's stable, riding and pasture areas should be neat and clean. Filthy stalls and rusty machine parts scattered around the pastures are indications that this is not an appropriate "horseman's university."

Ideally your initial lesson should consist of some instruction on how to work around horses: grooming, tacking up, safety tips, etc. These are important elements of horsemanship, so don't begrudge some time spent on them. But also remember you're paying to learn to *ride,* so don't allow such instruction to take up an inordinately large portion of every hour. A few (fortunately very few) stable managers use their paying customers as free grooms.

Early on, you may be put on a horse that is attached to a lunge line, or long lead rope. In this case, your instructor will control the horse on

A neat, clean and well-organized barn is a good indicator of responsible stable management.

a circle, leaving you free to concentrate on getting a good feel for the horse's rhythm and stride. You may be asked to ride this way without stirrups or bareback, or while doing various stretching, limbering or body-awareness exercises. With any luck, you'll find an instructor familiar with Sally Swift's centered riding techniques (see Recommended Reading, page 207).

It would be helpful for your lessons to include occasional trail riding opportunities. Few things better help a new rider gain balance and confidence—and break up the sometimes boring routine of riding in circles—than maneuvering a horse up and down hills, through water and over bridges and natural obstacles.

PAYING FOR INSTRUCTION/BARTERING SERVICES

If lessons are a financial hardship, perhaps you can arrange something with your stable manager. While teenage volunteer help is usually plentiful, many riding stables have a difficult time finding responsible adults who are willing and able to trade their services for riding instruction. Perhaps the stable needs an adult who can oversee the younger workers, or a groom, or a person who can drive a tractor and help with haying, or an exercise rider, bookkeeper, advertising copywriter or . . . You get the picture. Call on your imagination and experience to help you out here. Once your horsemanship improves beyond the beginner's stage— you and your instructor can decide when this time arrives—you may be able to serve as an apprentice horse trainer or assist with lessons.

A word of advice. While some "mucking out" chores are probably inevitable, given the sheer volume of body wastes that a stable full of horses produces, try to avoid this kind of menial labor as much as possible. Your goal is to be taken seriously as a horseman, novice or not. Let the kids do most of the mucking out. You're a dues-paying adult with a lot more to offer than a strong back.

If you make a working arrangement be sure that the responsibilities of both parties are clearly stated and understood. For example, your service hour is worth X amount of dollars, to be paid for through instruction and/or free-time riding privileges at the usual stable rates. Agree on what hours you are expected to work, and keep a written record of the time you put in. Have the manager or instructor sign this record each time you work. All this may seem picayune, but it helps to forestall misunderstandings and hard feelings, neither of which are conducive to good horsemanship.

If your service hours accumulate faster than you can use them on lessons, perhaps you can agree to "save" them for a later time when you might want to apply them toward boarding or training a horse, or even leasing or purchasing a favorite horse owned by the stable.

By now you've figured out that saving money is not the best part of this kind of arrangement. The best part is that you'll be gaining experience working around horses.

OTHER EDUCATIONAL OPPORTUNITIES

Don't limit your experience to lessons. Take every opportunity to be around and work with horses. Attend horse shows, preferably with someone who is knowledgeable about a show's specialization. Read about different kinds of competition, then attend every kind of show you can, whether it be breed-related, English or Western Pleasure, hunt seat, steeplechasing, dressage, three-day eventing, Western horsemanship, reining, cutting horse contests, draft horse pulling, driving, local 4-H shows—whatever. If you don't know anyone who can accompany you and help fill you in at these shows, keep your ears open for a friendly voice, and don't be afraid to ask questions. Inevitably someone nearby will be only too happy to help explain what's going on.

I've discovered that a remarkable fellowship exists among horsemen in general. Most experienced horse people are glad for the opportunity to meet and share information with other horse people, beginners or otherwise. This special quality is another reason why horsemanship is such a satisfying hobby.

Attend horse auctions. There you'll have the opportunity to evaluate horses and to find out what breeds are popular in your area and the price you can expect to pay. As an added bonus, you might be able to buy good-quality new or used tack at a reasonable price. Eventually you'll begin to recognize familiar faces in the crowd and observe how these individuals treat their animals. You'll develop a sense about who is trustworthy and who is not.

If you have a child who is interested in horses, inquire about the local 4-H horse club at your county agricultural extension agency. Attending 4-H meetings and shows with your child and helping him or her with horse projects will be a real learning experience for you! Through the 4-H office, you and your child will receive helpful educational literature and be informed of local stable and 4-H horse instruction clinics. And you'll meet other families who have an interest in horses.

RIDING OPPORTUNITIES

As soon as you've developed some confidence and stability in the saddle, you'll want to actually ride as many horses as you can. For responsible individuals, opportunities abound.

If you already live in the country and have a barn and pasture, perhaps you can board someone else's horse, offering reduced rates in exchange for riding privileges. Visit or vacation at a dude ranch or take a pack trip. Join a horseman's association or two, and avail yourself of every opportunity to borrow or rent horses from fellow members. Find out if neighbors or horsey acquaintances—perhaps a new mother, a full-time working mother or someone who travels—need a regular exercise rider. Once you've gained some experience, volunteer to spend time on young, or green, horses. Offer to work with the neighbor's horse who's been put to pasture while a horse-crazy youngster is off to college. If someone is an avid trail rider and owns more than one horse, ask if he would like company on the trail. Ask around at stables to see if the management or their boarders need an exercise rider. Once you ride well and have confidence in your ability, you might pick up some catch riding at local horse shows (in catch riding, a rider volunteers to show someone else's horse).

If you persevere, you should be able to work out a regular schedule of riding, just by creatively looking around and discovering other horsemen's needs. Don't make a pest of yourself, of course, but don't feel shy or guilty about offering to ride other people's horses either. At one time or another, many horsemen with other responsibilities would give anything to have the riding services of a serious, responsible adult.

Take sensible precautions when riding other people's horses, however. Always wear a protective helmet. Carefully observe the horse before mounting. Is he skittish? A little too bold or pushy? Has he been kept indoors, without exercise, for a prolonged period? Is he on a high-grain diet? This may produce excess energy. Perhaps he needs to be turned out or otherwise exercised for a while before you ride him.

Does the tack appear to fit the horse comfortably? If possible, have the owner or usual rider mount up and ride first, and observe the horse's manners and way of going. Always start your ride in an enclosed area—away from the barn, if possible. A horse that's rarely ridden or exercised or that's separated from his pasture mates might rebel when asked to move away from the barn under saddle. If this happens, remain relaxed but firm. Insist that the horse walk away. If he should prove to be too much horse for you, dismount and lead the horse a good distance from the barn before returning him to his stall. Explain the problem to the owner, and suggest that the horse might benefit from some retraining. A later chapter will teach you how to deal with such an animal, and you may want to take it on as a learning experience—but don't do so until you've had time to gain confidence in the saddle. A wily, spoiled horse is no training ground for a raw beginner.

On the other hand, don't underestimate your abilities. Once you've been at this a while and have taken several lessons, you may be able to cope with problems better than the horse's owner. If you've been riding many different horses, you've learned more than most people who ride only one horse. Such people may only ride three or four horses in their lifetime. You may do that easily in a month or in a week. You've learned about different breeds, their gaits and ways of going and their varying sensitivities toward people. You've discovered ways to deal with typical horse quirks, how to properly sit any type of saddle and the common differences between mares and geldings (let's assume your experience with stallions is sensibly limited at this point). You know whether you prefer an easygoing, shy-proof pleasure mount, or one that's sensitive and quick. A particular breed, possibly even a particular horse, has an irresistible appeal to you. You prefer a certain type of saddle and like to engage in one horse activity more than another. You're not happy to be up on just any horse, but enjoy a horse that offers some challenge or that has a certain way of going. In short, you know what you want and usually how to go about getting it.

Now it's time to buy or lease a horse of your own.

Three

CHOOSING THE
RIGHT HORSE

*F*ew experiences are headier than the process of buying or leasing your first horse. Although most people prefer to buy a horse, it might be worthwhile to check into leasing one. Leasing means you pay an agreed-upon amount of money per year or month for the use of the horse. In this respect it is like buying since you will usually be responsible for the horse's overall care and boarding, and have the animal to use as your own. One important difference is that should the animal prove unsuitable for some reason, you can return the horse to his owner without suffering further financial loss. Should you decide to lease a horse, make absolutely certain that all agreements—such as who is responsible for the horse in case of accidental injury or death—are in writing.

If you followed the advice in the last chapter and put off purchasing a horse until after you've gained experience with other people's horses, you're ahead of the game. You're acquainted with trustworthy people who can help you in your search. You know the kind of animal you're looking for and the uses you plan to put it to. You're confident in the saddle and experienced at riding different horses, and you can evaluate various animals' training, willingness, temperaments and riding gaits. Perhaps your riding has even led you to discover the perfect horse for you, making a time-consuming search unnecessary.

Sometimes it is not possible for the beginning horseman to get this kind of head start. Some areas lack stables that offer riding lessons. Or maybe you're uneasy about riding horses that are not your own. That's all right.

I don't think all beginners need the same qualities in their first mounts. This belief breaks all the rules. There's a saying among horsemen that when it comes to horses, a green rider and a green horse make a poor color combination. In other words, an inexperienced rider benefits most from an older, experienced horse, and an inexperienced horse needs a more advanced rider. While this is often true, sometimes green and green go together very well—with professional help and supervision. On the other hand, an experienced horse of a certain temperament may well outwit, bully or otherwise have a great deal of fun at the expense of the beginning or naturally timid rider. There's no magic formula that works for everyone.

Although it's a good idea to solicit the advice of experienced horsemen when looking at horses, only you can determine the qualities that make an animal perfect for your own use and enjoyment. In the end, you must trust your own judgment.

WHERE TO BEGIN YOUR SEARCH

There are literally dozens of places a person might look to find a good horse. As a rule, a horse auction is *not* one of them. While it's true that a good many perfectly acceptable horses are sold at auction, so are a great many more troublesome ones. Your chances of getting a good history on a horse, checking him thoroughly, having him examined by a veterinarian and trying him out in a suitable environment are all minimal at auction grounds. "Auction fever" can also set in, causing people to bid up an animal way past his true market value. At some auctions, horse dealers bid up the price of other dealers' horses to make it seem that all the animals are selling for high prices. In fact many horses that seem to sell for a high price at such auctions are actually "no sales." The prices on the floor may in no way represent the actual selling prices of the animals going to legitimate buyers. Bid in haste and you may indeed repent at leisure.

Disreputable dealers frequently misrepresent or drug animals and/or sell them with false registration papers. By all means, attend auctions for their educational and entertainment value, but unless something absolutely foolproof presents itself to you—and there's no such thing as a foolproof horse deal—purchase your horse elsewhere.

Look in the classified advertisements in your local paper. Regional swap sheets often have long listings of horse and horse-related items, as do regional and national horse magazines. I often save ads over a period of several weeks or months. When an ad on a promising-sounding horse

Though country horse auctions sometimes offer unusual horse-related items at a good price, be aware that many of the horses run through such auctions are unsound, overpriced—or dangerous.

no longer appears, I call to inquire if the animal is still available. If it hasn't sold after being advertised, chances are the owner will be willing to lower the price.

Word of mouth is an excellent way to hear about horses for sale. Just tell your horse-loving friends that you're looking for a particular kind of horse and what you're willing to pay. Some people make it a practice to keep an ear out for horses that sound promising and pass this information on to others who are looking for horses to purchase. Ask around to see if there are any reputable horse brokers in your area. If there are, using such a person's services can save you a lot of useless running around, as the following story illustrates.

We were looking for a big, easygoing trail horse for my husband. One classified ad sounded promising, so I gave the number a call.

"I hear you have an eleven-year-old Arab mare for sale. Can you tell me, is she the sort who really likes to move out, or would you describe her more as 'laid back'? " I asked.

"Oh, she's definitely the laid-back sort."

"I know Arabs aren't known for size, but my husband, who is over six feet tall, doesn't feel comfortable on a short horse. How tall would you say she is?"

"I'd guess she's at least 15.2 hands. I'm a big fella, and I used her for my trail horse," the owner assured me.

So far, so good. I made an appointment to see this "tall, easygoing, man's trail horse." The animal that struggled in from the pasture was barely over 14 hands high and so swaybacked that her nickname was Jelly Belly. She looked like something straight out of a cartoon.

Unfortunately, episodes such as this are common. I've often found it nearly impossible to tell from an owner's description what a horse is really like.

That's why it helps if there's someone who can screen potential purchases for you. Besides a professional horse broker, who usually charges a percentage of the horse's purchase price as a fee for services rendered, you can phone local stables, veterinarians and farriers, and ask if they know of any horses for sale that might be suitable for your needs. These people are usually happy to pass on any information free of charge. Check bulletin boards at the local tack shop. This may yield a wealth of horse-buying opportunities, and often there are photos of the horses tacked right up with the ad.

Above all, be patient. It's easy to get overly excited and impatient at this stage. After all, you're *finally* going to buy a horse of your own. It might seem like the sooner the better. Not so. Look at it this way: you've waited this long, so you might as well wait a little while longer to be sure that your first horse is the right horse. Besides, it's fun just to examine and ride different horses for sale.

HORSE SHOPPING

It is always a good idea to bring an experienced horseman along with you when you go horse shopping. Even if you are especially proficient at ascertaining a horse's character, or know bloodlines of a breed backward and forward, choose someone who has an acute eye for judging conformation. Such a person will add valuable insights of his own, confirm or challenge your impressions, and help guarantee that nothing important is overlooked during the evaluation.

There are many important qualities to evaluate when you look at

15

horses for sale. Under *no circumstances* should you purchase the first, second or even the third horse you look at. Don't buy until you've seen several, so you have some basis for comparison.

Price is often perceived as the most important horse-buying consideration. This is a shortsighted view since there is really no such thing as a cheap horse. The long-term costs of keeping a horse will soon outweigh your initial cash layout, and it will cost more, financially and emotionally, to keep an "inexpensive" horse with problems than it will to maintain a more expensive but trouble-free animal. For this reason evaluate horses in a variety of price ranges. Even though you must keep your costs within reason, you should be willing if necessary to stretch the budget to obtain a really good, suitable horse.

My husband and I learned this lesson after searching for many months for a family trail horse. We first decided how much we were willing to spend and looked at horses only in that price range. During this time I learned of a Tennessee Walking Horse mare for sale in our area, but refused to go look at her because the asking price was considerably more than we planned to spend. Then one day a friend, who was also looking for a horse, asked me to go with her to see this mare. I saw that horse and it was love at first sight. My friend decided this wasn't the horse for her, and I ruled her out as a possible purchase for our family because of the price.

After several weeks had passed, my husband and I were getting discouraged. None of the horses we looked at in our price range were appropriate to our needs. The owner of the walking horse telephoned me a couple of times, inviting me to bring my husband to look at the mare. She had already turned down one or two offers on the horse because she sensed the prospective buyers would not give her horse a suitable environment. Finally, my husband and I decided to go, "just to look."

My husband responded to the horse the same way I had. After all those months of fruitless searching, we realized we weren't going to find a more suitable horse, and so we hammered out a financial agreement with the owner. She was happy to sell her horse for less than the asking price to people who so obviously appreciated the mare's many fine qualities and who would give her a good home. We agreed to spend more than we had planned. Two years later, this is a decision our family has never regretted. When it comes to price, I urge you to keep an open mind.

FIRST IMPRESSION

Soundness

The first thing you will try to determine in your evaluation of a horse is whether or not the animal is sound. Unless a horse is essentially healthy and physically able to handle the weight of a rider, he's unsuitable as a using animal.

Begin by standing back and getting a general impression of the horse. Does he appear to be healthy, with a bright, interested eye and good overall muscle tone? Is he in good flesh, with no ribs standing out? Does he appear well balanced, so that his front and hind ends are the same height, his head and neck in good proportion to this body? On a well-built horse, everything ought to fit together well, with one area more or less flowing into another. A poorly built horse will break down under regular or hard use, and is likely to be uncomfortable to ride. (See Appendix I on conformation analysis for a more thorough treatment of this important subject.)

Your prepurchase observing should begin the moment the prospective purchase is led out. First impressions are important. Does the horse seem mannerly, with a bright, interested expression?

If the horse's body language says "look out!" you should pass the animal by. It is easier to overcome physical limitations in a horse than it is to conquer a bad attitude.

Is there any mucus running from the horse's nose? Are there any sores at the top of the withers, at the girth, or on any other area of the body? Do you notice any unusual white spots on his withers or sides that indicate he has been ridden with a poorly fitted saddle or that someone has been too free with spurs? These kinds of physical signs may offer valuable insight into the horse's psyche. A horse that's been ridden "sore" due to poorly fitted tack may prove sour or unwilling, and one that's been spurred too often or hard may have become numb to the rider's leg aids. Worn hair or white spots at the throatlatch may indicate the horse normally wears a cribbing strap. You can check to see if the horse is a cribber by having him stand with his muzzle over a board or rail of some sort. If he grabs on and sucks, then this had better be an outstanding horse in every other respect to make buying him worthwhile. (Cribbing and other bad habits are discussed in Chapter Twelve.)

How about his coat—is the hair long, dull and matted, or well groomed and shiny? Does he appear to favor one back leg or foot by resting it on its toe? Does he stand with his front feet camped out and pointed? Any of these symptoms may point to physical problems. (See Chapter Nine.)

Approach the horse and run your hands over him, starting with a very gentle touch and working up to a firmer one, especially over the withers, back, rump and girth areas. Does he wince, lay his ears back or otherwise signal pain or mistrust when you press on any given spot?

Evaluating the Horse in Motion

You can learn much about a horse by watching it move. Ask the handler to walk the horse away from and then back toward you, on even footing. Is the horse mannerly, neither lagging behind nor excessively pushy? Does the animal walk in a straight line, with long, even strides? Now have the handler trot the horse from you and back. Is there any noticeable pulling or catching of a hind leg? Watch the head. Does it bob evenly with every stride, or does it rise or duck more when a certain foot hits the ground? Are his strides smooth and long, or short and choppy? Does he carry his tail straight? A tail carried noticeably to one side may indicate back or hip problems. Do the horse's gaits look like they are smooth to ride, or does his back bounce up and down a great deal?

Handling the Horse While He Is Tied

Ask the handler to tie the horse so you can check his feet. "No foot, no horse" is an accurate saying. Tying the horse while you handle his feet is a good way to determine how mannerly he is. Some horses won't stand tied but pull back violently to escape any sort of restraint. It can be a nuisance to have such an animal in your barn. Others protest at having their feet handled. This makes it tough to get and keep a good farrier.

No matter what the owner claims, have him pick up the horse's feet before trying it yourself. Even then, stand close in to the side of the horse where you will be out of kicking range when handling his legs and feet.

The owner of an advertised "eleven-year-old, chestnut, AQHA mare" claimed on the phone that this was a great family horse. We went to look. I got suspicious when she led a bay rather than a chestnut horse out of the barn. Something about the horse's body language said, "Look out."

"Does this horse ever offer to bite or kick?" I asked.

"Oh, never!" her owner assured me. "She's just the sweetest thing. My eleven-year-old rides her all the time!"

Nevertheless, I exercised caution, and it was a good thing. I leaned into her back quarters and started running my hand down her leg, asking for her foot. She took a vicious sideways kick at me.

"Wouldn't you know a horse will make a liar out of you every time?" laughed her owner.

This woman didn't need the horse to do that. The only truthful thing she said about the horse was that it was a mare. A check of the teeth revealed that the mare was much older than eleven years. The registration papers her owner produced were evidently stolen from another horse, since neither the color nor the horse's age matched up with the information on the registration. I never even bothered to have the horse tacked up. No doubt, though, some poor unsuspecting buyer bought this woman's tale—and one loser of a horse.

Evaluating the Feet and Legs

You've seen the handler pick up all four feet and are now examining them for yourself. Is the horse well shod? With pads or without? If he has pads, ask why. Perhaps he's tender-footed, or there may be navicular (a serious unsoundness affecting the horse's feet), or some other problem. If the foot is padded or shod with a rolled toe, heart-bar or other kind of special shoe, your vet will want to pull a shoe to check the frog and perhaps even x-ray the foot before you decide to purchase.

Are the feet symmetrical and good-sized in proportion to the horse, so that the coronary band is at least as wide around as the fetlock joint? Are they well formed, without excessive "dishing" at the front? The frog, or sole of the foot, should be tough yet give to a firm touch. When the foot is picked out with a hoof pick, is there a strong foul odor, or can oozing material be seen coming from the cleft of the foot? Are there any cracks in the hoof wall? Ideally, the hoof should appear uncracked, shiny and almost translucent. Are the bulbs at the heels of the feet fully rounded and free of cracks and blisters? Is the coronary band unscarred and healthy-looking?

Now move up the leg. First, there should be sufficient bone. This means, simply, that the leg is big enough to support the horse and rider without breaking down. Ideally, a 1,000-pound horse who is going to be used for light jumping or regular hacks should measure between seven and eight inches around at the cannon bone just below the knee. Some breeds, such as Arabians, are especially tough, though finer-boned. Note any suspicious scarring, lumps or bumps in the pastern area. Check to see if the joints move back and forth and swing freely in a gentle arc.

Are the cannon bones, hocks and knees clean-looking, without noticeable swelling, puffing, scarring or lumpiness? Is the front knee flat, more or less shield-shaped and pointing toward the front when the animal stands square? Are the legs straight?

Keep in mind that a horse need not have perfect conformation to be a completely acceptable using horse. Few do, and those won't fit the budget of an ordinary mortal. Also, some conditions, such as capped hocks, well-healed splints and curbs and wind puffs, do not affect soundness, but you'll want your vet to make close examination if these kinds of conditions are noticed or suspected.

Handling the Head and Mouth

Check the horse's teeth. Do they indicate that the horse's age is being properly represented? (See Appendix I for information on ageing a horse.) Is there any foul odor from the mouth? Is the horse good-natured about having his head handled? A horse that violently throws up his head and stiffens his neck will likely be a handful. His actions may be a sign that the poor animal has been batted around the head, but it might merely indicate an extreme disdain for people. A horse that quietly offers you his head, with a bright, calm eye, is very likely going to be a joy to work around.

By now, you'll have some idea if the horse is mannerly when being handled from the ground. I should point out, however, that sometimes such a horse can prove to be a real spitfire under saddle. Conversely, some horses that seem especially hot when being handled from the ground become extremely docile under saddle. You need to make an all-around assessment, and decide what you can live with.

BUYER BEWARE

While evaluating the horse's soundness, you've been determining how easy he is to handle. You should also be talking to the owner/handler, checking his answers against information on the animal's registration papers and asking about the animal's background, experience and training. Your questioning might go something like this:

"How old did you say this horse is?"

"He's twelve last March."*

"Has he been ridden much lately?"

"No, not really."

"Why is that?"

"Well, my wife has had some health problems, and our daughter is off to college. I just don't have the time."

"When was he last ridden? Do you know?"

"Suzy rode him during the last spring break and said he went as though he'd been ridden every day."

"When was the last time he was ridden regularly?"

"Oh, let's see. It must have been a little over a year ago. Before Suzy went to school."

"How long have you owned the horse?"

"About three years."*

"Do you know who trained him?"

"Our neighbor down the road. He's trained horses all his life."*

"Would you mind if I talked to the trainer?"

"Heck, no—except he's moved out of the area."*

"Has the horse been used for trail riding?" (Or hunting, jumping, showing—whatever use you intend for the animal.)

"Sure! We trail rode every weekend."

"Does he get along with other horses? Or shy much?"

"Never had a bit of trouble. He can go all day." (You'll find, when looking at horses, that almost every horse being sold qualifies for sainthood.)

"You say he was ridden this last fall?"

"Yeah. Last fall."*

Now it's possible that this owner is completely honest, but note where I put asterisks in this conversation. First of all, when a horse gets to be twelve years old, it becomes more difficult to determine its age with any certitude. Therefore, if someone claims a horse is an "unregistered twelve- (thirteen-, or fourteen-) year-old," have a real expert check this animal's teeth. Also, although the owner says he's owned the twelve-year-old animal for a little more than three years, he claims that his "neighbor down the road"—who is no longer available for you to talk to—trained it. Did the neighbor own the horse, or was it not trained until it was nine years old or more? And notice that when you slipped in a question that inaccurately recalled one of the owner's statements, he didn't notice it but went along with the inaccuracy. It's easier to remember the truth than a lie.

While I don't want to suggest that everyone selling a horse is dishonest, you do need to be wary and perhaps even a little bit wily. Horse people who seem honest as pure gold often turn out to be otherwise. There's a reason for this. Horses are relatively expensive animals, both to buy and to maintain. When someone gets an unsuitable animal, they must decide how to dispose of it. Often owners decide to sell rather than suffer a serious financial loss. In order to get the best price possible and get rid of the animal, they cover up the truth—that the animal is getting too old, has developed respiratory problems, jumps into ditches when confronted by cars, kicks out at other horses or is simply too much horse for the rider to handle.

Who can blame them? Chances are good that somewhere in this world there is a person who will just love this horse despite the problems. Maybe that person is you. But, before making a commitment to purchase, you must do your best to determine what, if any, problems there are.

FURTHER PREPURCHASE ROUTINES

Tacking Up

If your impression of the horse's soundness is good, and you're happy with the kind of training and experience the owner claims for the animal, and he is an appropriate size, age and breed for your needs, then have the owner tack him up. Again you observe.

Does the tack seem to fit the horse? Does the horse offer his head, or at least not resist, when being bridled? There should be no sweating or nervous quivering when the saddle is lowered onto the horse's back, no cringing or laid-back ears when he is cinched up. These kinds of problems are the result of poor handling and usually can be overcome, but if the horse is unhappy at this stage, you'll know there *are* some problems to be dealt with.

Observing the Horse Under Saddle

Next watch the horse being ridden. Does he seem responsive to the rider? Will he take up a trot, then a canter, without tail wringing or other signs of a sour attitude? Is he easy to bring back down from these gaits? Does he seem to rush around, all hyped up and hot, or does he exhibit more of a steady attitude under saddle? What kind of bit is used—mild or severe? How tight does the owner hold onto the reins?

If the horse proves to be extremely difficult for the owner to ride, walk away. There are plenty of good horses to be had. Even if this horse is especially pretty or inexpensive, remember that "Pretty is as pretty does" and again, "There's no such thing as a cheap horse."

Riding the Horse

However, if he hasn't offered to buck hard, whirl, rear or bolt on his owner, go ahead and mount up, preferably in an enclosed area. Remember that most horses will be somewhat nervous under a new rider, just as most riders are nervous up on an unfamiliar horse. So start by asking for a slow walk. Once you've both relaxed, take the horse through his paces. Is he willing? Smooth? Does he have a good mouth? Is he responsive to your leg aids? Does he do everything the owner claims?

Next take him out in the open. Work him from walk to trot a few times. Is he still easy to stop? If so, then moving away from the barn, ask for a canter. Does he refuse or take the bit in his teeth in an attempt to bolt? Once he takes the gait, is he still easy to stop?

TAKE YOUR TIME WHEN DECIDING TO PURCHASE

If so far you like all of what you've seen and experienced, and you've tentatively decided this is the horse for you, then STOP! Don't allow the owner to make you feel hurried. Even if he claims six other people are just dying to buy this horse—a common ploy to pressure someone into making a quick decision—go home and think it over. Look at other horses. Stop back to check up on this horse at a time when you're not expected. There's always a slim chance that the animal was sedated on the day you originally went calling. See if his behavior on this visit is consistent with what you've already seen.

A MANDATORY VET AND LEGAL CHECK

If you still like the horse after all this, call your veterinarian to arrange for a professional vet check before making a financial commitment. If the owner of the horse is unwilling to allow the horse to be checked by a veterinarian of your choosing—never take the word of the owner's vet—then move on. This isn't the horse for you.

Another important point: You'll need to ascertain that the person selling the horse is in fact that animal's legal owner and has the right to sell. Ask the seller to show you the animal's current registration papers. Make sure the description of age, sex and identifying marks given on these papers match those of the animal you're interested in. The registration should indicate the name of the seller as the horse's registered owner. The seller should also be willing to sign a bill of sale and transfer papers for the animal immediately upon purchase, no questions asked. If there seems to be any discrepancy in the horse's description or the owner's name or a reluctance on the seller's part to duly record the sale, then back off the deal until all these matters are cleared up. Issues involving horse identity, legal ownership and rightful transfer absolutely must be in order before you commit to purchase a registered animal.

If, however, you like the horse, all the papers are in order and your vet gives you the go-ahead, then congratulations! You've just bought yourself a horse!

Four

ESTABLISHING A
SUITABLE
ENVIRONMENT

You've found the perfect horse. Now it's your responsibility to provide your new companion with an appropriate place to live. This isn't as hard as it may seem, nor as easy as careless horse owners like to think. While it's hardly necessary to keep your horse in a fancy stall, he won't thrive if he has to tolerate being confined to a small, dark rat-infested place.

A horse is a large animal, geared to grazing and running quickly from predators when the need arises. This means in his natural state he is either moving or ready to move at all times. It stands to reason such a creature, though domesticated, still requires plenty of opportunity to move around.

Ideally, this need will be fulfilled with a clean, well-lit and well-ventilated 12- by 12-foot box stall. This stall will open out onto a pasture or roomy paddock constructed of wood, high-tensile wire, electric wire or polyvinylchloride (PVC) fencing.

HOUSING AND TURNOUT

But we do not live in an ideal world. Neither, unfortunately, do our horses, so we all have to compromise. While a 12- by 12-foot box stall is ideal, one that measures as little as 9 feet by 9 feet will suffice—as long as the horse has room enough to turn around or lay down without getting cast, or caught, against the walls of the stall when he attempts to roll or get up. If this much space is not available, then a tie or standing stall, narrow enough so the horse won't try to lie down and roll, may be acceptable if he isn't forced to face a blank wall and *he is provided with daily turnout and/or other exercise.* This last point cannot be stressed too strongly.

It's nothing fancy, but this lucky mule enjoys good facilities for any equine: safe high-tensile fencing, shelter from flies and the elements and room to roam.

Actually, though a tie stall intensifies the need for regular exercise, every effort should be made to guarantee that the horse gets sufficient turnout and disciplined exercise regardless of stall size. In the best of all worlds, a horse will be turned out to good grass pasture every day, along with a couple of herd mates. He will also be actively exercised for a minimum of one hour several times a week.

If this sort of routine is not possible, come as close to the ideal as possible. If pasture is scarce, use a paddock or riding arena for turnout. If neither of these is readily available (a truly sorry state of affairs for the horse), you must ensure that the animal is exercised every day. This can be accomplished either by riding, or by lungeing. (See pages 134–139 for a discussion of lungeing.)

If you discover after purchasing your horse that providing adequate exercise is impossible, then sell the horse. I say this without apology. Regularly keeping a horse in a tie or box stall twenty-four hours a day constitutes abuse. Even more than people, horses are simply not equipped physically or psychologically to thrive in extensive isolation and confinement.

In fact, it is better for a horse to have too much turnout than not enough. Let's imagine, for example, that a woman has a trail horse gelding she keeps outdoors in a roomy pasture all the time, in good weather and bad, with nothing but a small shed and the bodies of other companion horses for shelter. She keeps an expensive show mare in a well-lit, well-ventilated 12- by 12-foot box stall. The mare is groomed daily and well fed, but is never turned out and seldom ridden, except during the short show season.

The gelding is far better off. His living conditions are closer to what is natural for horses. He actually has all that a horse needs to thrive—an abundance of good grass hay, room to romp, a few friendly companion animals and shelter from bad weather. In fact, this may be what horse heaven is like!

The mare, on the other hand, is no better off than someone serving an interminable sentence in solitary confinement. In fact, she may be worse off than such an inmate. She hasn't done anything to deserve such punishment. Her natural body rhythms and energy levels—not to mention the high-energy feed she probably receives—continually agitate her to keep moving. She doesn't read or watch television, and has no "occupational therapy" or "work detail" to occupy her mental abilities.

Is it any wonder that some horses kept in this manner eventually become known as outlaws? Their frustration and energy levels build to such an extent that handling or riding them becomes risky.

This is primarily why stallions have such a poor reputation. While stallions may be innately more volatile than mares or geldings, it is also true that because of zoning ordinances and to keep them away from neighboring mares, a great many of them are fed high-energy rations and kept confined to stalls. They are allowed out only for breeding purposes, if then. When the animal becomes unmanageable, it is chalked up to the horse's gender rather than to the cruel treatment he's endured. I've ridden with people whose stallions are as mannerly and enjoyable as any mare or gelding. Invariably, these animals are given regular turnout and the companionship of herd mates.

Even sadder than the overstalled outlaw is the horse who becomes depressed when kept confined. Such an animal's problems are seldom recognized and addressed. In fact, his behavior may be deemed desirable since he gives his owners little trouble. His depressed lethargy is mistaken for docility and tractability, and his slow, plodding gaits have actually become the ideal for some breeds of pleasure show horses. Those who have promoted this kind of thinking perhaps ought to be tied in a standing stall for a few months in order to have time to reevaluate their position.

If an overstalled horse doesn't become fractious or depressed, it is almost certain to develop other behavioral problems. Such stable vices as cribbing, weaving, pawing, stall kicking, wood chewing and windsucking (each explained in Chapter Twelve) are generally associated with animals that have been kept in close confinement. Sadly, these stable vices usually remain even when the animal's circumstances change for the better. How much easier and kinder it would be if the bad habits were never fostered.

So, I repeat, be certain you can provide your horse with daily turnout and/or exercise. If not for your horse, then do it for yourself—as a rule, a contented horse is a true pleasure to own.

FENCING

Earlier it was suggested that pasture or paddock fencing be constructed of wood, high-tensile or electric wire, or sturdy PVC. Although these materials are initially more expensive than barbed wire, the latter should be your last choice for horse pastures.

When trapped, horses tend to panic. When accidentally trapped in barbed wire, more than one animal has pulled and seesawed in a frantic attempt to get loose, until they either damaged themselves badly enough to necessitate euthanasia or bled to death. Few things are more horrible than going out to the pasture to discover a horse with its leg nearly sawed off on barbed wire.

Wood fences are safer than barbed wire but may be expensive to keep up. Upkeep costs depend largely on your horse's habits. Some horses like to lean on wood fencing until it falls over. Others chew the wood or just stand around all day cribbing.

PVC fencing, while expensive to purchase and install, is less expensive to maintain than wood. It is also attractive and relatively horse-proof, and can add to the value of your property. About the only real drawback to this kind of fencing, aside from its initial cost, is that it tends to become brittle and crack in very cold climates.

Barbed wire, though inexpensive, can be a dangerous choice for horse fencing.

High-tensile wire fencing is an excellent all-around choice for horse pastures. While not inexpensive, it costs less than PVC, and usually no more than wood. It is long-lasting, easily maintained and safe to use around horses. Should you decide to use this material, make certain that the person installing it sinks deep posts and good, well-braced corner poles; the high tension of these fences necessitates the extra-strong bracing. There should also be a minimum of four strands of wire strung. If less than four wires are used, a smart horse may maneuver his way right through the fencing, one wily foot at a time.

Then there's electric wire fencing, which is less expensive than wood and offers the benefit of mobility, as an enclosure can be taken down and moved to another field with a minimum of effort. Also, horses pastured with electric wire tend to be respectful of fencing. I've seen wire fencing fall down—one of the drawbacks of electric wire—and the pastured horses refused to cross over even the fallen wire. There are now a number of types of electrical sources available—solar, ac/dc and battery—each with its own set of costs, benefits and drawbacks. You'll want to investigate these options carefully before committing to a system.

PASTURE SAFETY

Safe fencing is only one element of pasture safety. Though pasture-run horses are generally more surefooted than their stalled counterparts, and therefore less likely to fall or stumble, small animals can leave burrow openings nearly hidden along fence lines and in tall grass. Natural ground movements tend to work large rocks to the surface. Because these holes and rocks pose a hazard to a horse carelessly frisking around the pasture, make it a habit to walk your pastures regularly with a wheelbarrow and spade. Remove rocks and use them, with dirt, to fill in holes. If field pests become too persistent (not likely in a pasture, since the large animals' presence tends to scare them off), consider getting a dog to help keep them chased off. Just make sure the dog isn't one that likes to run or harass horses.

STALLS

Now back to the barn. Although some people allow their horses free run in and out of their barn—and this is a nearly ideal situation—it is usually unworkable when you have more than one or two horses. The reason is that dominant horses will run their herd mates out of the barn, just to prove they can do it. The less-dominant animals end up braving the cold and getting the last pickings of hay and grain. Besides this, the handling required for bringing an individual horse in and out of its stall each day is good for the horse and good for the handler—it facilitates a relationship. So plan to provide a stall for your horse or horses.

You may wish to purchase and install a stall system from one of the commercial businesses that offer such things. Usually, these come complete with heavy-duty finished plank-wood walls, doors, grills and sliding-door tracks. They also come with a hefty price tag.

If you decide to build your own stall from scratch, remember the size considerations mentioned earlier. Avoid using plywood for the stall walls, as one kick can easily splinter even half- or three-quarter-inch-thick plywood and possibly destroy your horse's leg. Avoid composite wood materials, such as wafer board, as horses may chew on the edges of stall materials and the adhesives in these materials can be harmful. Even if the horse doesn't chew, some binding materials exude carcinogenic gases that cause respiratory distress in horses.

Stall walls should be built with heavy-duty pine or hardwood planks. These are placed together to form a solid wall, or at least close enough together that a horse won't accidentally get a foot caught between them if he kicks out. Gates may be built in the same way, with good sturdy hinges and latches. Sliding-track doors, though more expensive, offer the greatest space benefits. These also aren't as likely to be rushed or pushed through by a horse anxious to join his buddies outdoors, and track doors offer the handler a bit more control when entering or exiting the stall.

Grills, or heavy-duty steel-mesh screen, may be placed at the top, between horse's stalls. This screening prevents the physical back-and-forth bickering—and ensuing property damage—that transpires among horses, yet it allows for good ventilation. Horses kept alone generally do not benefit from this sort of isolating material. In fact, many well-mannered horses get along just great together without any kind of stall separators. You'll have to decide for yourself what works best for your particular animals.

If you don't use mesh or grill fronts on your stalls, make certain that all harmful tools and barn materials are way out of the horse's reach—and horses have a long reach, perhaps as much as five feet. Equines can discover unique ways to entertain themselves with stable forks, lead ropes, grooming sprays and carelessly hung scissors, hoof picks and bridles. Grain must be stored in a safe, out-of-the-way place—preferably locked in a separate tack or feed room. Horses that get loose with a bag of grain will overeat, colic, founder—perhaps even die.

STALL FLOORS

Horsemen have tried for decades, if not centuries, to come up with the perfect floor and bedding combination for horse stalls. The ideal stall floor system leaches moisture through, traps droppings underneath, doesn't compress too easily, insulates the floor for warmth, offers good footing, is resilient, is neither palatable nor harmful to horses and is easy to handle.

Many horse barns, particularly commercial establishments, have concrete stall floors. Concrete is suitable for stables that have many horses passing through, as it makes it easy to clean and disinfect the stalls, thereby cutting down on disease. However, concrete is suitable only if the stalls are deeply bedded, and it is not the best solution for the home barn. Concrete, as a rule, is too unforgiving and slippery a surface for horses. Providing enough bedding to make it acceptable will prove to be expensive and time-consuming; concrete is cold, tends to make bedding material mash and does not leach moisture from the stall. Horses that routinely lie down on poorly bedded concrete are apt to develop abrasions and capped hocks, an unsightly and possibly uncomfortable blemish. The same holds true for asphalt, stones and brick.

Wood flooring, on the other hand, is perfectly acceptable and, though expensive to install, will last for years. It is slippery when wet, so requires deep bedding, but it offers excellent resiliency. When installing a wood floor, treated hardwood planks at least two inches thick are the ideal. Leave one-inch gaps between the boards for drainage and to accommodate shrinking and expanding wood.

Natural dirt floors are prone to become saturated and full of potholes. They also hold ammonia odors, which are bad for a horse's respiratory system. Though I prefer floors of natural ground materials, they must be well planned and executed to work well. I elaborate on this below.

BEDDING

While your stall floor is a once- or twice-in-a-lifetime investment, you'll find yourself dealing with bedding materials on a daily basis. You can afford some trial and error here, until you find a bedding that meets your needs.

Straw, of course, is the old standby bedding, and it does an admirable job under most circumstances. Some horses like to eat straw bedding, which encourages parasite infestation and may prove expensive. Wheat straw is generally preferable to rye, barley or oats. If you use wheat or rye straw, be sure all grain has been threshed out, as horses can founder from eating ergot, a toxic fungus that develops on these grains.

Don't make the mistake of substituting hay for straw in an effort to cut costs. You'll be doubling your workload and providing your horse with a wet, messy, smelly, eminently *edible* stall. Hay is superabsorbent, and its long fibers mat easily. Picking it up when wet and matted is back-breaking.

Other materials commonly used for bedding are sawdust, wood

shavings, sand and, recently, ground peanut shells and shredded paper. Less-orthodox new materials include rice hulls mixed with other materials, such as wood shavings, and a new paper-pulp material.

Sawdust, while usually inexpensive, must not be too dusty or it may prove a hazard to your horse's respiratory system. Even the coarser grades should be sprinkled down to prevent inhalation. Like hay, sawdust tends to saturate and compact down very easily, making some spots in the stall particularly wet. When cleaning wet spots, a great deal of bedding must be disposed of, which adds to your workload—and long-term costs. All in all, it's acceptable but hardly ideal.

Wood shavings are another story altogether. Available by the truckload or the bale, kiln-dried or not, they can be a very good bedding material. A stall that is deeply bedded with shavings will stay dry and warm from the ground, and will cushion droppings so they don't mash down. This may sound trivial, but such droppings are easy to pick up with a stable fork so you don't have to throw a lot of mashed-in bedding out with the droppings, which saves money. Horses generally won't eat shavings, and if they should ingest some, it passes through their systems without harm. One word of caution: Make sure there are no black walnut shavings in your horse's bedding. Black walnut shavings cause founder, a disease that can prove fatal to your horse.

Sand can be a workable bedding, but it too has drawbacks. While it keeps stalls reasonably dry, it is a poor insulator. Also horses can develop colic from accidentally ingesting sand, so if you use it, make doubly certain feed isn't eaten from the stall floor (easier said than done).

Ground peanut shells provide many of the benefits of wood shavings but aren't available in every region of the country and can be expensive. They also may be dusty.

With recycling, baled shredded paper has become the bedding of choice for many horsekeepers. Recycled shredded paper has proved easy to handle, inexpensive, unpalatable yet harmless to ingest and a good insulator. Although it saturates, the wet spots don't condense as badly as sawdust or hay, so that droppings and wet spots are relatively easy to isolate and pick out. Add to this the fact that it is an ecologically sound choice, and shredded paper certainly offers many advantages.

The more unconventional rice and paper-pulp products that have come onto the market may be worth investigating. They are easy to handle, compost quickly, and are dust-free, an especially good feature if your horse suffers from heaves. One major drawback is the limited availability of these products. If interested in them, check with your local agricultural or veterinarian supply company.

A COMPREHENSIVE SYSTEM

The flooring and bedding system I've come to prefer is one in which materials are installed in several layers. First, the stall is dug out to a depth of one to three feet, depending on the percolation values of the subsoil under your barn. If your barn has extremely poor natural drainage, your base material will consist of several inches of large stone or rocks. This layer is covered by several more inches of crushed stone or creek-run gravel. If your barn has naturally good drainage, the stone or gravel will be your base layer. On top of this material goes a 6- to 12-inch mixture of sand and clay (30/70 ratio). Clay is used rather than plain dirt because clay is solid enough to offer good footing and it resists developing potholes. The added sand is to facilitate drainage. Finish by laying a deep (6- to 10-inch) bedding of wood shavings and then a shallow layer of straw or shredded paper.

Though setting up this system may sound like a lot of work, the savings in time, money and energy are considerable over the long run. When the horse eliminates, wet spots go onto the top bedding and droppings work down into the shavings, where they are prevented from getting mashed. If you are reasonably conscientious about cleanup, the heaviest-wetting horse (and horses pass gallons of urine daily) will not be able to saturate this stall. Any moisture the straw or paper doesn't absorb is passed through the shavings and through the sand/dirt mixture to the gravel bed below, from which it leaches out through the ground. Cleaning such a stall entails little more than scooping up a few forkfuls of wet paper and some intact droppings, then replacing the paper. The wood shavings have to be supplemented only once or twice yearly.

FLOOR FOR THE PAWING HORSE

If your horse has the habit of pawing, he can wreak havoc on even the best-planned natural stall floors. Happily, there is an alternative to installing a solid floor of wood or concrete. Before installing the top 6 inches of gravel, lay two lengths of treated 2- by 6-inch lumber flat on top of your base layer of flooring, so they line up along two opposite parameters of the stall. On top of these lay rows of treated 2- by 4-inch lumber across the stall floor, leaving 2 to 3 inches of space open between each piece of lumber. Securely bolt the ends of each 2 by 4 to the lengths of 2- by 6-inch lumber laid beneath them. Now fill the spaces between the lumber with gravel till all the wood is covered, leaving a shallow layer on top. Top with usual bedding materials. This extra work should save a lot of long-term aggravation: When your horse starts digging, his foot hits the edge of the lumber, which prevents him from digging up and ruining the stall floor.

WHAT TO LOOK FOR IN A BOARDING FACILITY

You may have to board your horse out, rather than keep him at home. You will want to be as conscientious about stalls, fencing, pastures, bedding, feed and feed storage, exercise and other matters as you would be if you kept your horse in a barn of your own. In addition, there are a few other considerations when deciding where to board your horse.

Be certain that the person or people who board your horse are knowledgeable about horses. While a dairy farmer or neighbor may offer a better price for pasture board than the local horse stable, will that person know that if your horse is standing with his front toes pointed out in an awkward position or lying down and rolling too often, it means he should get veterinary help on the double? Horses have very particular needs, and you must make certain that the person overseeing your horse will recognize and meet them.

Who will be responsible if your horse is accidentally injured at the stable? You or the stable owner? Is the stable insured against such accidents? Will it recommend the services of a competent veterinarian and farrier, and make sure these people are called if you or your own service people cannot be reached in an emergency? A properly run establishment will not allow other people to ride your horse without your specific permission. Make certain your tack and grooming supplies will be kept in a clean, dry area and are secure against other peoples' use and abuse.

Are there nearby trails and/or good arenas available for use? Does the stable offer riding lessons or horse hauling? All these services might

If you board your horse at a local cattle or dairy farm, be certain the farm management is knowledgeable about horses and that pastures are not over-crowded or overgrazed.

not be necessary, but you should determine which ones are important to you. The facility needs to be within easy commuting distance of your home, or you and your horse may end up virtual strangers. Be certain responsibilities and obligations are clearly spelled out, and make sure there are no hidden costs. Talk with other boarders, to see if there are any recurring gripes. Also, by talking with other boarders you'll get a feel of how well you will fit in at the stable.

More important than how well you like the other boarders is whether or not you and the stable owner or manager see eye to eye on major horse-management issues. If you are of the "patience is better than force" school of horsemanship, you are bound to run into difficulties if the stable owner uses strong-arm tactics. It's often hard, particularly if you're a relative novice, to stand up to such people (note I didn't refer to them as horsemen). They'll insist you're being "soft" and "spoiling" your horse, which may make you feel you'd better start getting tough or make you overly defensive.

37

More important than the way you feel in this sort of situation is the way your horse will start behaving—or misbehaving—if handled inappropriately. Horses must be handled with authority, consistency, tact and sensitivity. Ascertain that a correct balance concerning such issues is maintained at your boarding stable. Learn from others who are more experienced, yes—but also learn to trust your own judgment.

Wherever you decide to keep your horse, the care and well-being of that wonderful animal rests squarely on your shoulders. There are no good excuses for poor horse management.

Five

GETTING TO KNOW

YOUR HORSE

Your dream has come true—almost. You've found a magnificent horse, negotiated hard, purchased him, made appropriate living arrangements for him, and a friend or local professional has hauled him home. You've installed him in his new roomy, airy stall, enticed him with choice tidbits and lovingly groomed him an hour every day for a week.

The only thing wrong is that he pointedly, and at every opportunity, ignores you. You've noticed that, unless you've got a grain bucket in your hand, he can barely tolerate your company. Your efforts to establish a good rapport by softly rubbing his crest or nose are met by a hard eye and fiercely raised head. While you groom him he tunes you out, obviously lost in thoughts of his own.

Don't be discouraged. Horses generally do not demonstrate affection as quickly or in the same way that a dog or other domestic animal might. They're independent. Some horses, particularly those who have been mistreated at some time (and many have been), take several months to form strong attachments. Like people, some never are very demonstrative, while others are real pets right from the start. Horses also lack the muscles that would enable them to exhibit affection through facial expression. We need to learn to read their body language. Be patient. With time and practice you will learn to generate and recognize your horse's responses of affection.

HAND FEEDING

First of all, though a horse will look forward to his feeding times, and thus to your presence at those times, don't expect him to "love" you

At first it may seem that your horse pointedly ignores your every attempt to be friendly.

merely because you provide him with food or treats. Remember, horses are by nature grazing animals and naturally expect a continual source of nourishment to be present at all times. You wouldn't expect your horse to "love" the ground just because it provides him with grass, would you? Of course not—in fact, he walks all over it!

And that's what he'll do to you too, if you try to win your horse over through the dispensing of hand-held tidbits. Constant feedings are extremely counterproductive. Your horse learns to associate your presence with food and eventually has nothing but eating on his mind every time you work with him. Constant feeding leads to an unpleasant, grabby, spoiled horse, to say nothing of an obese one.

THE FIRST DAYS HOME

When your horse first comes home, allow several days for him to become accustomed to his new surroundings. Horses are creatures of habit and strong attachments. Even if his previous living conditions were less than optimal, it will be several days before he begins to adjust to new ones. If at his previous home he was strongly attached to another horse or human—even a stall—he may pace, cry and go off his feed for the first twenty-four hours. A mare thus distressed may suddenly go into heat, creating additional turmoil in the barn. Some horses, rather than acting agitated, become lethargic. This, too, is a normal response and must be met with understanding and patience.

On his first day home, keep your horse within sight and sound of other horses in the barn, but do not allow him actual physical contact with those other horses. If there are no other horses in the barn, make every effort to provide some kind of companionship for him—a goat, a barn cat or dog can all be acceptable substitutes. If this isn't possible, then take extra time out from your schedule to keep him company—at least an hour or two each day for the first several days. When you can't be with him, provide company in the form of a softly playing radio (but make sure all electrical cords and devices are placed well out of his reach).

After the horse has been settled in his stall with plenty of good-quality hay for two or three hours, take him out, with halter and lead rope, for a walk around his new pasture, making sure there are no other horses out there to challenge or excite him. Lead him by walking at his shoulder, not ahead of him, and keep close enough to his side so that if he should decide to throw a happy buck, you won't get kicked. Don't let him lead you around or push into you, but insist with voice and lead rope and arm that he walk at your side while keeping a respectful distance.

Show him the pasture's parameters, teach him where to get a drink of water and where to find a spot of shelter from the sun or wind. Allow him to be curious, to sniff at everything, to enjoy a roll if he wants. If he rolls, stand well back and keep the lead above his head, so his feet don't get tangled in it and you don't get pulled into his antics.

If your horse isn't used to turnout, he may have a lot of pent-up energy to dispose of. In this case, use a long rope or lunge line for a lead, take him out to an enclosed area and lunge him until he's settled down (lungeing is covered in Chapter Ten). If you have never lunged a horse, have someone experienced give you a hand. As a last resort, turn him out by himself for an hour or two. The biggest problem with this is that some horses are hard to catch and you want to avoid any confrontations on your first day together, if possible.

A GOOD GROOMING ROUTINE

After an hour or so, bring the horse back to the barn and begin your grooming routine. The first few times you groom your horse you will certainly want to tie him, but eventually you will be able to leave his head free while you work. While you are grooming him, teach him not to eat or move around. Keep all feedstuffs out of the area. If he moves, calmly apply pressure to his side and say "step." Don't lean into him with all your might, or he'll tend to lean back. If you poke at him with annoying little jabs, he might blow up. Apply firm pressure, using a give-and-take motion, and say "step" each time you do so. Eventually a horse will move away from this kind of pressure and step back to his original position. When he does, say "stand" and reward him with a pat, but there's no need to get all gushy just because he did what he should. Be consistent, and he'll quickly learn what's expected of him.

This simple exercise teaches a horse much more than you might imagine. It teaches him to respect your rules, authority and space, to move away from pressure, to reposition his feet when you say the word "step" and to stand still when you say "stand." You are beginning to build a relationship built on mutual respect and understanding.

Start your grooming routine with a rubber curry comb, using a circular motion to work up dander, encourage circulation and loosen old hair. Once the horse has been well curried, go over him with a stiff-bristled brush, brushing in the direction his hair lies. Don't neglect the inside of the legs, under the tail, the neck and the belly. Then, if you have time, go over him with a soft dandy brush. When time is short, at least use the dandy brush carefully over his face. Then take a damp rag or sponge and wipe around his eyes and under the dock of his tail. If your horse is a mare, occasionally use a clean damp rag to gently wipe out the waxy substance that collects between her udders. A gelding may need his sheath wiped clean.

Talk to your horse as you work, watching his expressions and his subtle body language. If his back flinches as you go over it, use a lighter touch (and a heavier saddle pad when riding). If he lays his ears back and looks menacing when you reach under to groom the girth area, be aware that he may have suffered a great deal of distress in that spot over the years. Use a firm but sensitive touch, reassuring him with your voice as you work.

At all times stay out of harm's way, and do not under any circumstances allow your horse to bully you. Wear hard boots to protect your feet. When working on his hindquarters, stand in close to one side rather than directly behind him. When you must move behind him, move in very close with a firm hand on his rump, and talk to him so your actions don't startle him. Don't suddenly just jump around the back of him; instead move with calm, steady purpose. When you move in tight behind the horse's back legs, all he can do if he tries to kick is push you away. Moving out two or three feet from the back of the horse gives his foot just enough space to gather momentum and do real damage. In fact, this area is known as the kill zone.

If your horse swings his head menacingly in your direction, quickly and calmly reach up and push it back, and say "quit." If he raises a hind foot, swat the upper part of his leg and say "quit!" Using the command "quit" is better than continually saying "whoa," as the latter means "stop moving your legs," and the former, spoken with authority but no shrillness, is easily understood by your horse to mean "stop whatever you're doing!" If your horse is already standing still, he doesn't need to be told to stop moving his legs. The simple command "quit," rightly used, can help avoid a lot of human/equine misunderstandings.

If your horse seems surly or threatens in any way, don't walk behind him at all until you can fully trust him. Never walk under the neck of a tied horse, either, or you may be struck by his front feet if he suddenly panics and rears or pulls back. If you need to go around from the front, unhook the horse, command him to "back," and walk in front of his head. If certain grooming actions draw a negative response, don't labor the point. Move on to something else until his relaxed gaze and lowered head tells you he's enjoying your touch.

At no time during your sessions should you pick on your horse by concentrating too long or too often on his more sensitive areas. The idea is to slowly and subtly accustom him to your all-over touch until he's learned to trust you. This will only happen over time, after you've proved yourself trustworthy.

Horses are generally more sensitive along the top middle portion of the back, along the girth line, along the back portion of their underbellies, and around their ears and polls. Use a firm but gentle touch in these areas. Also be especially careful when currying or brushing the lower legs, where the skin tends to be thin.

Horses often enjoy being scratched or curried along the crest and

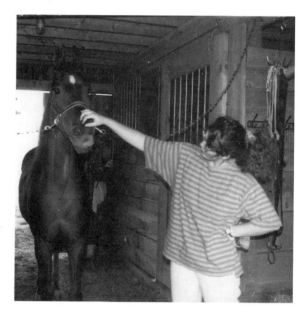

It's fun to discover a streak of playfulness in a horse, but playtime is no substitute for regular, overall grooming.

the sides of the neck, along the edge of the withers (though some horses have pain in this area, so be careful), along the back and tops of their rumps, and on their chins, lips, jowls and faces.

When you start brushing or rubbing a spot that feels especially good, your horse may lift his head, curl his lip and make dreamy eyes at you and the ceiling. Or his head may drop and his eyes droop. It's fun to watch him enjoy himself, but remember that scratching "special spots" on your horse is no substitute for a good all-over grooming—and also remember not to allow your horse to move his feet, even when he's totally immersed in pleasure. He must respect your space, and your rules, at all times. Otherwise, you'll end up with an animal that gets too pushy, that swings his hind end into you or uses his head to butt you around as he tries to indicate the spot he wants scratched. This behavior stops being cute the instant it results in someone being pushed down or trampled, as it almost surely will sooner or later.

Once you've finished brushing your horse, comb out his mane and tail using a wide-toothed comb or special mane-and-tail brush. Brush out from the ends to the top to work out tangles.

 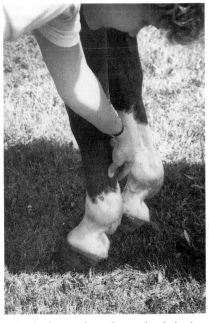

To lift horse's leg, lean into the horse while running your hand down his leg. This action causes horse to shift his weight in preparation for standing on three legs.

Pinch the tendon above the fetlock to get the horse to lift his foot.

ROUTINE CARE OF THE FEET

Now comes the part that gives some horse people a lot of trouble. It's time to pick up, and pick out, your horse's feet.

Start at the front left, facing the horse's rear. Grasp your horse's leg just above the pastern, lean into him to shift his balance, and say "up" at the same time you firmly pinch on either side of the tendons just above the pastern joint. This causes a horse to reflexively lift his foot. Once the horse's foot is up, don't allow him to put it back down of his own volition. If he does, repeat the pattern until you can hold the foot a few seconds and set it back down yourself. Again, don't try to accomplish everything overnight. Holding the foot a few seconds and setting it down is better than fighting for an hour for control of the horse's foot. He'll give you more, in time.

If you will always work the hoof pick in a direction pointed away from yourself and the horse, sudden movement won't cause injury.

When he allows you to hold the foot, take your hoof pick and, keeping the pointed edge directed outward, away from yourself and the horse, use the point to work any bedding or other matter out of the clefts on the sole of his foot. Work until the frog, or horny part of the sole, is completely cleared of mud, manure and bedding and you can see the sole of the foot around the edge of the frog. Set the horse's foot down carefully, to avoid injury to the toe of the foot.

Move back to the left rear leg. Still facing backward, lean down and grab the rear leg at the same juncture above the pastern as you did the front foot. Again, lean into the horse, pinch the tendons behind the lower cannon bone and say "up." Repeat the cleaning procedure.

Work your way counterclockwise around the horse, establishing this pattern as a routine. Before long, your horse will calmly anticipate your next request and offer you each foot in turn. This may seem difficult to believe at first, especially if your horse is stubborn about having his feet handled. Often such problems result from early inappropriate training or handling, but they are easy to overcome with patience, a calm attitude, tact and a little knowledge.

CLIPPING THE BRIDLE PATH

Another common grooming technique you'll need to master is that of clipping a bridle path—something that must be done regularly for the comfort of your horse and the sake of your riding. An unclipped mane puts unwanted "padding" between the bridle at the poll, dulling whatever effect it has. It also will tend to tangle in the crown piece of the bridle, causing discomfort.

Buy good-quality animal clippers. Before you begin clipping, cross-tie your horse. Ask him to lower his head and carefully clip away a 3- to 5-inch section of mane, beginning just behind the poll and working back toward the withers. How long a path you clip will depend upon the current style of your horse's breed, but clipping one ear's length is a good rule. Within a very short time most horses will stand quietly for this procedure.

If your horse balks at the sound or feel of the clippers, expose him to it gradually. Start by merely running the clippers in his presence for five minutes at a time. Once he's accustomed to this, move them closer. Soon you'll be able to lay the back side of the clippers against his muzzle. Once he tolerates this, move it on up to his poll and start to work, using slow, deliberate movements and talking quietly.

WHY GROOM?

What do you and your horse gain from such a grooming routine? For starters, it helps you to get to know one another. It generates mutual respect and trust. It creates a physical bonding, and you and your horse learn to relax and enjoy one another's company. A sensible grooming routine establishes your authority while reinforcing habits of obedience in your horse. It predisposes a horse to be mannerly when being handled by vets and farriers. Grooming also keeps your horse looking good, while you get some physical exercise. And it gives you the opportunity to regularly check your horse for signs of disease, parasite infestation, wounds, sore spots and loose shoes. It's impossible to overestimate the importance of regular grooming.

TURNOUT

After the first day, you'll want to turn your horse out loose in a pasture or paddock for exercise. If he's an "only child," this will be a simple matter: Just turn him out and watch him for the first few minutes to be certain he doesn't panic and run into a fence. If he's to be pastured with other horses, this step becomes more complicated.

Horses establish a definite pecking order within the herd, and it's almost impossible to tell what order in the hierarchy a horse is assigned until you observe him with other animals. Often horses who seem aggressive toward humans are lower on the pecking order than more phlegmatic individuals. The first few days a horse is turned out with another horse or horses, there will be some squabbling until herd rank is established. Count on it. But you can also be sure that, if handled properly, no horse needs to be seriously injured.

Your horse will probably start out low in the herd. So the first time he's turned out, send him out with a low-ranking horse. Give them a couple of days to get to know one another by turning them out together. Once they're getting along, add another horse to the mix. After a day or two, add another and so on, until it seems your horse has been accepted and found his niche in the herd.

If your horse is kept with more than three or four other horses and turnout space is limited, see to it that the horses are not all turned out together at the same time. Horses need their own space; if they don't get it, serious fighting may result. If sufficient turnout space is a problem, there should be a limitation on the number of animals turned out at any given time. In effect, different "herds" are established. This may actually be necessary in cases where there are only four or five horses but two are so dominant that neither acknowledges the leadership of the other.

If after two or three days it seems obvious that fighting is becoming more rather than less serious, or if the initial fighting consists of two horses facing off and landing some truly nasty bites and kicks, with neither horse backing off, then by all means split those horses up. Carry a long whip out to the pasture with you, and use it aggressively to split up the horses. Be careful not to get in the center of a fight. On the other hand, if one horse runs, walks or backs away from aggression after being challenged, be certain they'll work things out without your intervention.

ESTABLISHING A WORK ROUTINE

I don't recommend riding your horse the first day he comes home to live. Give him a day or two to settle in. But don't wait longer than that to get him started to work. You don't want him to think he's just a pampered guest; if that happens, he may rebel when you finally ask him to start earning his keep.

Regular riding is good for a horse. It keeps him mentally and physically sharp. Have you ever noticed in your own life how laying off physical labor or exercise for even a short period makes getting back to the work doubly hard? But engaging in regular physical activity makes it seem easy, even pleasurable. So it is with your horse. If you ride him often, he'll enjoy the experience. If you seldom ride, he'll be balky and difficult to handle. An added complication is that you'll also be out of practice and insecure. What I've seen happen again and again is that when a horse becomes difficult, the owner rides less—which only makes the horse more difficult and the owner less willing and able to handle him.

For your own sake as well as your horse's, determine to ride at least three times a week. If that's impossible, try to find an experienced person to ride for you on a regular basis, just to keep your horse willing and sharp. If problems crop up, work them out. Don't be afraid to ask for help.

Follow this advice and your mount will soon be a true pleasure to ride, what is commonly known as a push-button horse. Many people seem to think these kinds of horses come by their abilities naturally, that the owner or trainer has had little or nothing to do with it. But don't you believe that. The truth is that push-button horses are never born; they are developed through the steady application of a sensible routine.

Six

BASIC RIDING

"*H*orsemen are born, not made" is a common adage. While it's true that some people possess unusual sensitivity to animals, and others are born with an especially good sense of rhythm and still others enjoy athletic ability—and all of these play an important role in fine horsemanship—no one is really a "born horseman." The only way to become a proficient horseman is to take the natural inclinations we have, gain as much reliable knowledge as we can and then diligently apply our newfound knowledge to practical situations. So, paradoxically, a horseman is neither born nor taught. The learning required to become a good riding horseman takes place both in our head and by the seat of our pants.

Which is all by way of saying: Get thee onto a horse!

A RIDING PLAN

In the last chapter I encouraged you to ride at least three times a week. Even better advice is to ride every day. The more riding you do, the better you'll become. Some people are better riders after only one year of experience than are others who have ridden their entire lives. Successful horsemanship hinges not on simply being around horses nor even upon a great deal of riding. It results from obtaining reliable knowledge and proving that knowledge through plenty of practice.

This book is not the best place to learn basic riding skills. Your initial lessons ought to be under the tutelage of a sympathetic, experienced instructor. The information contained here is intended as a supplement to personal riding instruction. Only a good instructor can make correct judgments about your progress and help you make appropriate adjustments. Good riding is much easier if we start out with good habits than if we learn incorrectly; when that happens, we have to unlearn bad habits before replacing them with good ones. It's also very difficult, if not impossible, to judge our own seat, hand, leg and body positions. What may feel perfectly upright and balanced may in fact be quite out of kilter because we are naturally "one sided." A one-sided rider will never bring out the best in a horse and indeed may cause the animal a great deal of discomfort. So for your own sake, as well as your horse's, plan to invest in some riding lessons.

OVERCOMING NERVOUSNESS

The first thing you must learn, and practice, when saddling and riding your horse is calmness. This attitude comes naturally to some people but is harder for others. If you're nervous around horses, take heart; with time, you will develop the ability to be truly calm. Meanwhile, fake it. If you feel shaky, take several deep breaths before handling your horse. Keep your voice low-pitched when talking to him. If your mouth gets dry, suck on a mint. When you aren't in the saddle, daydream about being in the saddle. Envision yourself as calm: You do everything correctly and your horse responds perfectly to your every cue. Shut out every negative fear that enters your mind and replace it with a positive idea.

When you're not riding under the eye of an instructor, ride with a more experienced friend, one who will communicate confidence, because confidence is catching. Another thing that helps conquer nervous energy is exercise. A twenty-minute walk, a bicycle ride or ten minutes of aerobic dancing before riding releases nervous tension from the body and clears the mind of fears. It sharpens your thinking, physical sensitivity and reflexes.

Some nervousness is natural for beginning riders, but you must not allow it to overwhelm you. If you discover that in spite of your best efforts you are nearly overcome by fear or nervousness around horses, don't despair. It happens to many of us at one time or another. Persevere, get the kind of help you need and follow the advice given above. If you tend to be especially nervous around horses, be sure the horse you choose has a placid, honest temperament and plenty of experience. Such an animal will help a nervous beginner overcome many hurdles, not the least of which is lack of trust, the main impetus behind fearful riding.

MOUNTING

To ride, you've got to be able to get on top of a horse. While television and rodeo cowboys spring lightly up into the saddle, without stirrups or apparent exertion, and young children just scramble up the horse's side, chances are your early efforts to mount will require just that—effort. Like anything, it becomes easier with time.

Instructors often teach riders to stand on the near, or left, side of the horse with both reins held in the left hand, facing the back of the horse. Then, with your left hand, you take hold of a piece of the mane at the horse's neck just above the withers, lift your left foot and, using your right hand, twist the stirrup around and place your left foot in it. Next, still holding both reins and the piece of mane in the left hand, grab the pommel of the saddle with the right hand, and lightly swing around and up from the ground into the saddle.

This is, strictly speaking, the correct way to mount a horse. And theoretically it makes sense. The thinking here is that, should the horse move forward when you put your foot in the stirrup, he'll be moving toward you, and you can easily use his forward momentum to help you swing up into the saddle.

Perhaps in time you'll be able to do just that. But it's not practical to expect this sort of well-coordinated, acrobatic feat from a less-than-agile, inexperienced adult. Some horses, having learned that being mounted means a heavy weight being suddenly and painfully thumped down onto their backs, instinctively jump forward as soon as the rider's weight is placed in the stirrup. If your horse moves forward at this point, you'll find yourself with your left foot hung up in the stirrup, hopping backward to keep up with your horse's forward movement. You'll need an awful lot of "heave ho" to generate enough energy to leap lightly forward onto your horse's back from a hopping backward position.

"Lightly" is the important word here. Above all, you must cause your horse no discomfort upon mounting. Even if you are fairly agile, this will probably mean that you should mount from a face-forward position.

First, make certain your horse is standing with all four feet well under him, so your weight won't pull him off balance. Standing in close on your horse's near side, facing diagonally forward toward the horse, take both reins in your right hand. With your left hand, pull the reins through your right hand until very light contact is established. Shorten the right, or far-side, rein slightly more than the near-side rein, so the horse's nose is tipped slightly away from you. If the horse does move, his body will swing toward rather than away from you as you mount.

Now lift your left leg, and place your foot in the stirrup. Keep the inside front of your calf and the knee of your left leg in contact with the side of the horse, with your body in as close as possible. To avoid having your toe swing in and jab the horse's side as you lift yourself up, place the toe of your boot firmly against the girth. Grab the pommel with your right hand, the horse's neck just above the withers with your left. Command your horse to "stand." Bounce up from the ball of your right foot. As your weight leaves the ground, stiffen and straighten your left leg in the stirrup. The instant you're standing upright in the stirrup, transfer most of your weight to your arms. Now lift and bend your right leg high over the horse's rump, being careful not to bump his croup. Sit down lightly into the saddle. Position your right foot in the right stirrup. Step firmly into each stirrup to recenter the saddle on your horse's back.

This may sound complicated, but it is actually accomplished as one smooth move and it's not hard to master. The most important thing is, again, not to thump down heavily onto your horse's back. It's also desirable not to pull or tug the saddle way out of line as you pull yourself up, or tug your horse off balance. To prevent this, make the horse stand with all four feet squared under him when you mount, stand as close as possible to your horse when mounting and mount as quickly as possible.

Avoiding causing your horse pain may mean, at least for a while and especially if you are a heavy person or have a weak upper body, positioning your horse beside a secure mounting block and mounting from there. Some people dismiss this sort of device, pointing out that mounting blocks aren't available out on the trail. That is not strictly true. If you must dismount and remount in a place where there is no mounting block, ask for a leg up from a companion. Or look around to find a spot where you can stand your horse in a slight decline, enabling you to mount him from a higher elevation. Position him at the base of a tree, while you stand up higher on its root base. Perhaps there's a shallow ditch he can stand in while you mount from above. Tree stumps, truck bumpers and large rocks can all serve as emergency mounting

Stand in close to the horse's near (left) side. Keep slight contact with the reins in your right hand to maintain control.

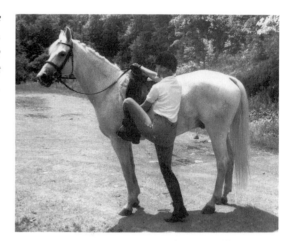

Grab the horse's mane just above the withers with your left hand, the saddle pommel with your right. Bounce up on the ball of your right foot. Stiffen and straighten your left leg in the stirrup and immediately transfer the bulk of your weight to your arms.

Swing your right leg over the horse, being careful not to bump his croup.

Step into both stirrups to reposition (straighten) the saddle; then settle lightly into the seat.

To dismount safely, swing your right leg over the croup, then pull both feet from the stirrups and vault to the ground. Leaving one foot in the stirrup and stepping down may result in entanglement and injury if the horse suddenly moves.

If you have any difficulty mounting, use a secure mounting block.

blocks. If you are careful never to hurt your horse when mounting, he should be happy to stand still for mounting wherever you wish to stand him. Gaining even a couple of inches advantage will make mounting much easier. As you mount regularly, your muscles and coordination will improve so that eventually you can dispense with the mounting block.

If your horse insists on moving off while you try to mount, see page 52 to learn how to handle this problem. But remember, the best way to handle a problem is to avoid it in the first place. In this case, that means never causing your horse pain when you mount. If this requires the use of a mounting block, then ignore any ridicule or advice to the contrary, and do what's best for your horse—which means *you* are the better horseman.

BALANCED RIDING

Now you're in the saddle. No matter what kind of saddle you ride— English, Western, Australian or any other—there is a basic rule to follow regarding your seat, or riding position. Your center of balance, which is at a point slightly above and behind your navel, should be carried over your horse's center of balance, located just slightly behind the girth area,

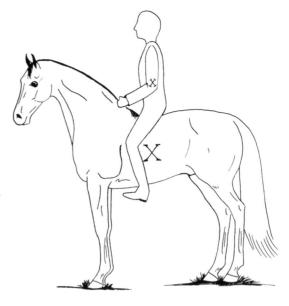

The rider's center of balance, which lies approximately behind the rider's elbow in this illustration, should form a straight line with the horse's center of balance. Note that a straight line could be drawn through the rider's head, shoulder, seat and heel.

Regardless of riding style, the rider's center of balance must be positioned over the horse's center of balance.

Though the horse's center of balance at the canter, or lope, is naturally farther forward than at slower gaits, a well-trained horse under a good rider moves in a more collected frame, so that his center of balance remains constant. This improves the horse's way of going, as well as making him lovelier to watch and easier to ride.

As the horse's speed increases to a gallop, the center of balance is shifted forward, so the rider rises slightly out of the saddle and leans forward. This action brings the rider's center of balance in line with the mount's and prevents his or her seat from bouncing painfully on the horse's back.

57

mid torso. When your horse is standing still, it's easy to obtain this ideal, provided you have a well-fitted and balanced saddle. Simply sit straight and relaxed so that your head, torso, seat and feet fall in a straight line about four inches behind the elbow of the horse, just behind the girth. Your shoulders should be upright but relaxed, your elbows carried close to your side, your leg slightly bent at the knee. In the stirrup, your ankle is relaxed, your toes pointed slightly up, heels down. Once you feel you're in the correct position, look down. If you can see the toe of your foot past your knee, it is too far forward and should be moved back.

As the horse moves forward, his center of balance shifts forward and so must yours. On a moving horse you must synchronize your body's balance and movements to your horse's balance and movements. Learning to ride in harmony with your horse takes knowledge and practice. Many people merely become "passengers" and never learn to become active, thoughtful riders. Good riding is reflected through the movements of a horse, so that even a less physically talented animal improves under a good rider. "Passengers" produce horses that have a clumsy, graceless way of going.

RIDING EXERCISES

There are exercises you can do that will quickly help you gain a sense of security in the saddle while teaching you how to feel, and follow, your horse's movements. Most of these exercises require a helper. Your riding instructor may take you through some or all of them, or you may do them with a friend. Some can be done on your own. These exercises will dramatically shorten the time it takes you to gain a sense of unity with your horse.

EXERCISE #1.   If your horse is a very quiet individual, you may do this exercise on your own. Otherwise, enlist a helper to hold your horse's head.

Seated in the saddle, without stirrups or reins, lean your body back as far as you can on the horse, so your head rests, or nearly rests, on his croup. Your legs may lift forward. Once you're as far back as you can go, relax your legs back down as far as possible. Maintain this position for ten seconds, breathing deeply and relaxing your muscles. Sit up. Repeat five times. Now lean forward as far as you can go, till your

Touching your toes from the back of a horse helps increase your agility and security in the saddle.

forehead rests on your horse's neck. Lift your legs backward. Hold this position for five seconds, then lower your legs and sit up. Repeat five times.

EXERCISE #2.   Seated in the saddle, reach down with your right hand to touch your left ankle or boot. Now sit up. Reach down with your left hand to touch your right ankle or boot. Repeat five times to each side.

With an assistant leading your horse at a walk, repeat the exercise.

EXERCISE #3.   While your assistant leads your horse at a walk, stretch both hands high over your head, breathing deeply. Now move them in a windmill motion, attempting to match your forward strokes with the opposite side forward step of your horse's front foot. For example, as your horse's front right foot steps forward, your left hand rotates forward. Have your assistant cue you to "right, left, right, left," until you get a feel for the footfalls yourself. As you rotate your arms, your seat shifts in the saddle in synchrony with the rolling motion of the horse.

Windmill motions with your arms, synchronized to the horse's footfalls, will help you increase your feeling for the animal's movement.

EXERCISE #4.   Do this exercise with an assistant. You are on the horse, with or without a saddle, but without reins or stirrups. At a standstill, sit tall. Lift your knees straight up the sides of the horse, so that the tops of your upper legs are parallel with the top of the horse's back. Hold lightly onto the pommel for support and lean your upper body back slightly. Now drop your legs down and straighten your upper body, but keep your seat bones in the same position as when your knees were raised. You are now neither leaning back onto the rear part of your buttocks nor forward onto your crotch; rather you are balanced on the rocker-like seat bones between. This is the deepest, most secure way to sit a saddle.

Close your eyes, and concentrate on the feel of both relaxing and lengthening your legs. At the same time, imagine a string being drawn from the deepest part of the saddle, up through your torso and neck, and out through the top of your head. This string is being held by a puppeteer, and you are held upright by it. Take deep, slow breaths, lengthening your legs with each intake, lifting your torso higher with each inhala-

To obtain ideal seat-bone position, raise your legs even with the top of the saddle . . .

. . . then lower them, maintaining the same position with your seat as when your legs were raised.

tion, so that, without tension, your spine and ribs are being lengthened. Imagine your weight falling into your heels, your upper body becoming lighter with each breath. Your hands rest lightly on the front of your upper thighs; your elbows are in at your sides.

Keep this position and do five shoulder rolls, back to front, then front to back. Now *very* slowly roll your head in a complete circle, twice in each direction. Imagine the puppeteer's string again, and adjust your posture accordingly.

Still breathing deeply, have your assistant walk your horse steadily in a straight line. Lightly pull yourself up on the saddle pommel when you slip out of position. Otherwise, keep your arms and hands relaxed.

Close your eyes and concentrate on the feel of the horse's movements, your own breathing and the sound of the horse's footfalls. Practice this until you can lose yourself in these rhythms. At this point, you will be moving with the horse and balancing easily.

Ask your assistant to lead the horse in a figure eight, so that you're circling smoothly in both directions. Again concentrate on the sounds and sensations, and on balancing lightly over your horse's center of balance. You will lean ever so slightly forward as he begins to move forward. As the horse circles to the right, you will take more weight on your right seat bone, while lengthening your left leg for balance. With your eyes closed, you won't be able to anticipate your horse's actions, but you will be able to feel the effect his movements have on your balance. You are programming your body to respond to physical, rather than visual, riding cues. This ability makes for faster, more correct riding reactions.

EXERCISE #5. You are ready for work at a sitting trot, or jog. Balancing lightly now is more difficult, as your horse's motion is more up and down than it was at a walk. You will need to soften your back to absorb the up and down percussion. Concentrate on softening your back and breathing deeply; with each intake of breath, naturally lift the muscles of your lower abdomen.

With your horse on a lead or lunge line, practice the sitting trot, at first with your hand on the pommel of the saddle—not holding tightly, as that will cause your body to stiffen, but using just enough grip to help maintain a balanced, secure position in the saddle. Avoid gripping the sides of the horse with your knees, as that motion tends to push you up out of the saddle, your upper body becoming heavier and more rakishly balanced and your legs becoming "shorter" and less secure on the barrel of the horse. Sit deeply, lengthen your leg and grip the horse's sides only with your calf when you need to grip. Limit this exercise to five- to ten-minute periods, as it is tiring for both rider and horse.

Riding your horse without reins or stirrups at a sitting (or slow) trot is the most valuable riding exercise you can perform. There's no substitute for it. Whenever you ride your horse, even when an assistant isn't available, practice riding at a slow trot, without stirrups on a loose rein, for a few minutes. When you can maintain good balance at the sitting trot using a flexible, relaxed seat and calves alone—without bouncing all over or forcing yourself to stay in place by the use of pinched knees and tight reins—you will have attained a good measure of security in the saddle and are well on your way toward harmonious riding.

LEARNING CONTROL

Well-balanced security in the saddle is the first half of good riding. The second half is having control of your horse. Simply having control is no measure of a horseman, however; the manner in which he gains and maintains control is equally important. It should be subtle. A rule of thumb is a rider should use the least amount of pressure possible to obtain obedience from his horse.

THE AIDS—NATURAL AND ARTIFICIAL

A rider's basic means of control are called aids. Natural aids consist of voice, legs, hands and seat. Artificial aids include the riding crop and spurs.

The voice is used to give commands and to encourage and reprimand. At first it may be used often, but it becomes less important as the rider increases his proficiency at using his body to direct the horse.

A horse's energy for forward motion, or impulsion, comes through its powerful hindquarters. The rider uses his legs to urge the horse's hind end forward, in a movement called generating impulsion. The rider's hands on the reins are used to control, or check, forward impulsion. Horsemen are continually admonished to keep a horse "between the rider's legs and hands." Legs generate forward movement; hands control it.

A good rider should not need to depend on a severe bit to control the horse.

This does not mean we *kick* a horse to get him to move forward and *yank* on his mouth to get him to stop. Quite the contrary. Our legs communicate only as energetically as necessary to get the forward motion we need, and no more. Constantly booting a horse in the ribs only makes a horse ignore the pain we inflict. As we intermittently squeeze our legs on his sides only as hard as necessary and then release the pressure the instant he moves or speeds up, we reward the horse for responding promptly to our cues, and he learns to obey promptly.

Likewise, we must never pull on a horse's mouth or we will end up with a head-tossing, hard-mouthed, unruly horse. It's best to keep light to moderate rein contact when riding and to keep contact steady by having our elbows at our sides and permitting our hands and arms to move in unison with the horse's head motions. This is known as having "soft, following hands." Good hands are a much-desired trait among horsemen.

To stop, our legs urge the horse forward, while our hands (or wrists, actually) refuse to "give" to the head's forward motion. Thus the horse's body is literally squared to a stop as his energy flow is caught "between the rider's legs and hands."

If a horse refuses to move forward despite our urgings, then our aids become stronger, perhaps even to the point of the quick use of crop or spur. But if a horse is "hard-mouthed," the answer seldom lies in using

The correct way to hold English reins. A subtle downward bend of the wrist or tightening of the fingers should be all that is needed to effectively communicate with the horse.

The correct way to handle Western reins.

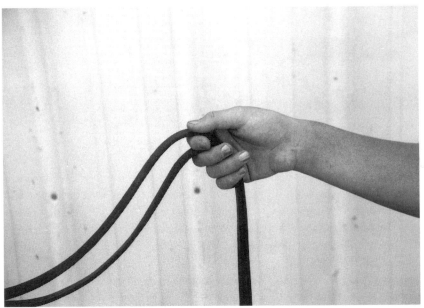

a more severe bit or greater pull on his mouth; these methods only exacerbate the problem. A better approach is to work on making the animal more flexible and responsive. We will discuss particulars on how to accomplish these goals in Chapter Twelve. For now, your aim is

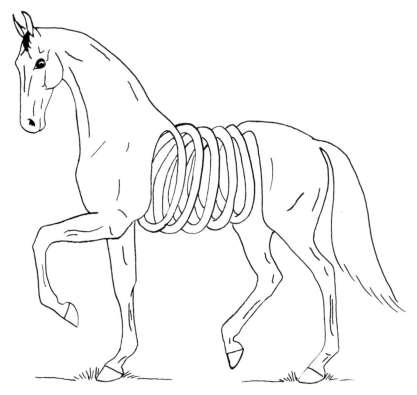

By visualizing the horse's torso as a spring, it is easy to see how a rider's aids influence the horse's way of going and responsiveness. If the rider is a mere passenger, allowing the horse to stretch his body out and move in a dispirited manner, the spring becomes saggy and the ride bouncy, uncoordinated and uncomfortable. When however, the rider uses his or her legs to generate plenty of forward energy, then "captures" that energy through the rein, the spring— and horse's frame—is condensed. In this state, the ride is springy and comfortable. A correctly executed half halt produces a tightly coiled spring effect, causing the horse to be ready and able to spring immediately forward or backward in response to the next riding cue.

always to teach the horse to respond promptly to lighter and more subtle aids.

The hands, reinforced by the seat and legs, are used to indicate and maintain direction, and to check forward impulsion. When you generate impulsion with your legs and then check it through the use of hands and seat you are executing a half halt. The hand aids are communicated through the rein, and the rein should run in an imaginary straight line from the horse's mouth to the rider's elbow, again held close to the rider's side. The seat communicates through the use of balance, through forward urging and through resistance.

Here's what all the above means in practical terms.

TRANSITIONS

The Half Halt

You should practice this important riding maneuver until you understand it well and use it consistently. The half halt consists of squeezing the legs to increase impulsion while checking the energy thus generated through subtle resistance in the seat and hands. The purpose of the half halt is twofold. First, it requests your horse's attention. You're saying, in effect, "Listen up, I'm about to ask you for something." Second, it condenses his energy, so that his body could be likened to a coiled spring held between your legs and hands, ready to be released in either direction. When the horse's energy is thus held, he is said to be collected.

For an upward transition (stop to walk, walk to trot, trot to canter), lean forward and give the horse more encouragement with your legs and less resistance through your hands so that his collected energy springs forward. For a downward transition (canter to trot, trot to walk, walk to stop), stiffen your back and seat, lean slightly back, relax your legs and offer greater resistance with your hands. Now the horse's collected energy is shifted backward.

Walking

To begin your horse walking: Half halt. Squeeze lightly with your legs. Follow his head movement, with your hands maintaining light contact.

Walk to Trot

For an upward transition from walk to trot: Half halt. When your horse's gait slows slightly and his ears flick backward to tell you he's listening, quickly give a sharp squeeze with your legs at the same time you move both your hands and your upper body slightly forward. Say "trot," if necessary, but dispense with this vocal aid as soon as possible.

This method is much preferable to simply urging the horse into such fast forward action that he falls into the trot. That kind of uncontrolled trot will be bouncy and hard to sit. Besides, you want to be the one controlling your mount's gaits.

Fast trotting under saddle puts a lot of stress on your horse's back. His legs move as diagonal pairs—right front and left hind forward on the ground, then left front and right hind forward. There is a moment of suspension between the time one diagonal comes up and the next pair of legs hit the ground. Whenever there is total suspension from the ground, there will be a percussion upon landing, as jumping just a little ways up in the air proves. This means there will be some jarring as each diagonal set of legs makes ground contact. So the rider, no matter how well balanced, will bounce in the saddle. The more energetic the trot, the greater the bounce.

Posting the Trot

To lessen the impact of the rider's weight on the horse's back at the fast trot, we post the trot. Posting involves lifting your weight up out of the saddle as one diagonal set of legs lands, then lowering your seat back into the saddle as the next diagonal pair strikes the ground. When you post, the horse suffers your weight landing on his back only half the time; when you do land your weight is less jarring on his back than it would be if you simply sat in the saddle and bounced because, when you post your ankles, knees and back serve as shock absorbers.

To Post: Trot. Using the thigh muscles and straightening the knee joint, lift your pelvis up and slightly forward, toward the hands—but be careful not to pull yourself up using the reins. Sit gently back down by relaxing your thigh muscles and bending your knees. Avoid lifting your-self up by pinching your knees together, as this creates tension and prevents your joints from being able to absorb shock. It also pops you up out of the saddle in an unbalanced, top-heavy position and prevents

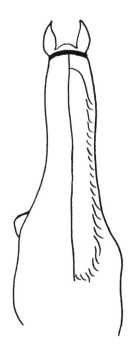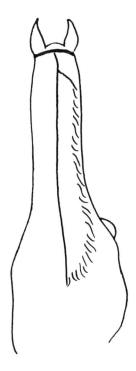

Posting should be done by feel. When the horse's hind leg comes forward, it will literally lift you up out of the saddle. On a circle, the inside hind, or impulsion, leg moves farther forward and more vigorously than the outside hind leg, thus making the action more pronounced and easier to post up from. To verify if you are on correct diagonal when posting on a circle, check the horse's shoulder. The shoulder that is bulging forward indicates which leg is moving forward to make ground contact. When the outside shoulder is bulging (left illustration) you should be rising out of the seat. You should be lowering yourself back down on the seat when the inside shoulder bulges (right illustration).

you from giving good lower-leg aids. The horse's rear-back motion will naturally tend to lift you up out of the saddle, and, with practice, you'll find yourself posting up and down easily.

At the trot, you can see which front leg has ground contact by looking down at the horse's shoulder. The movement of the horse's leg rotates his shoulder. The shoulder that is rotated forward (the most bulging one) indicates which foot will swing forward to make ground contact next. For best weight aid when posting the trot on a circle, rise out of the saddle as the horse's outside front leg begins its forward arc. Sit back down as the inside front leg swings forward. This lightens the weight on your horse's inside hind impulsion leg, which helps the horse generate energy in that direction. This is called posting on the diagonal.

Though you must post either the right or left diagonal in any case, it matters little which one you use when on the straightaway. However, you should change diagonals from time to time to avoid overtaxing one side of your horse. Change diagonals by either sitting or standing one extra beat of the trot.

Cantering

Horses canter on both the left and right leads. This means when the horse is circling or moving toward the right, his feet coordinate and land in such a way that he is well balanced to the right; his weight is shifted so that the greatest portion of weight is borne on the right side of his body. The right front foot lands farther ahead than the left front foot while the right rear foot lands farther ahead than the left rear foot. To imagine how this works, stand up and walk in a circle to the right, bringing one foot up only as far as the other, never past it. Note how the right inside leg is the one you naturally use as your "leading" leg. Now try to walk the same circle to the right, using your left leg as the front, or leading, leg. Feels unnatural and off balance, doesn't it? It will to the horse, too.

The canter on the right lead follows this three-beat cadence: left rear, left front and right hind, right front, then a moment of suspension. The order is reversed for the left lead.

Just as you would, a horse will naturally take the correct lead for the direction he's traveling. But when you place a rider on the horse's back, his balance shifts. He may take the wrong lead. This motion, called countercantering, causes an uncomfortable, unbalanced ride.

Horse cantering on the left lead.

Horse cantering on the right lead.

When the horse takes different leads, front and back, he lapses into a disunited or cross canter.

It is your responsibility to coordinate your and the horse's mutual balance so that it is easy for the horse to take the correct lead. You can most easily accomplish this mutual balance by lightening the weight over the horse's leading front leg; you should slightly tilt the horse's head in the opposite direction from the one in which he's traveling. Your weight is then shifted to your inside stirrup and seat bone so the horse tends to move in under you, while you maintain only slight contact with your inside leg and move your outside leg behind the girth. Push with your outside calf so the horse's hindquarters are pushed in the direction you want him to take. The force of impulsion coming from the outside hindquarters pushing over the lightened inside shoulder will cause the inside front leg to spring forward to catch the weight, and the horse has taken a correct lead.

Many horsemen and instructors will take exception with the above advice about tipping the horse's head to the outside when asking for a canter. This advice is intended for the person who is learning to ask for a canter, not necessarily for the more accomplished rider. A new rider's balance is such that his mount needs all the deliberate mechanical help he can get to assist him in taking the correct lead. As you gain experience, you certainly should begin to ask your horse for a balanced canter using more subtle body aids, and you will be able to correctly position your horse's head to face the direction of travel. Until you can do this easily, however, my best advice is to stick with what works.

To canter on the right lead: Half halt. Shift some weight to the right stirrup and seat bone. Move your left leg slightly behind the girth while tipping your horse's head slightly to the left. Push energetically with your seat and outside left leg while releasing resistance on the reins. Reverse this sequence for the left lead.

Speed Transitions

To increase speed while staying at the same gait (from a slow to a fast walk, for example): Squeeze with your legs while giving the horse his head.

To decrease speed at the same gait (from a fast to a slow trot, for example): Maintain the same pressure as before with your legs, and offer less give with your hands.

As with any other skill, riding control is developed in stages. At first, you'll be doing well just to get your horse to stand, start, stop and turn when you want. Later, you'll ask for up and down transitions. As you gain knowledge and experience, communication between you and your horse will become more instantaneous, subtle and varied. The ideal is to learn to operate with your horse almost as if the two of you were a single entity.

MAINTAINING REALISTIC GOALS

Regardless of your specific riding goals, harmony between horse and rider is the overall ideal. You may aspire to become a world-class dressage rider or to win blue ribbons at local or national horse shows. Your greatest pleasure may be in quiet moments on the trail, when you and your horse stop to watch deer grazing, or when he takes up a lovely, soft canter almost as the desire to canter crosses your mind. Allow yourself any goals you like. But give yourself plenty of time to learn, and be sure your goals are suitable for you personally by regularly checking your measure of pleasure.

To enjoy the horse, a certain level of proficiency is necessary, but we needn't become Grand Prix dressage riders, professional trainers, horse show heroes, rodeo riders or Olympic contenders. When we become overly demanding, competitive or ambitious, or when we get too caught up in lofty theories and ideals about horsemanship, our relationship with the horse tends to cease as a labor of love and becomes merely laborious.

Seven

TACK AND

EQUIPMENT

Tack is the term used to describe any equipment that is tacked on or appended to a horse to facilitate using the horse. Tack refers to saddles, pads, bridles, halters, harnesses and other use-related items.

Just as there are many styles of riding, there are also many kinds of specialized riding tack. The equipment you choose will be determined by your personal riding goals, as well as by the type and training of your horse.

Take time to choose your riding gear wisely, as unsuitable tack hinders good riding and may cause discomfort for the horse, possibly to the point of rebellion. A mistake can be financially costly, because good quality tack is expensive, and poorly fitted or otherwise unsuitable equipment must be replaced as soon as possible.

Basically, there are two categories of riding styles and corresponding tack from which all others originate: English and Western. Saddles in both categories are built on a frame, or tree. Saddle trees are made of wood and/or metal or, with some Western saddles, fiberglass; they are heavily padded and covered with leather. The ideal saddle, regardless of style, conforms to the shape of the horse's back and helps protect it. The seat should be of a size and shape to fit the rider well. A well-made, well-fitted and well-maintained saddle will give you years of comfortable, secure riding.

ENGLISH TACK

Saddles

The English saddle category includes dressage, hunt seat, saddle seat and all-purpose saddles. All types of English saddles have a sleek, sloping

74

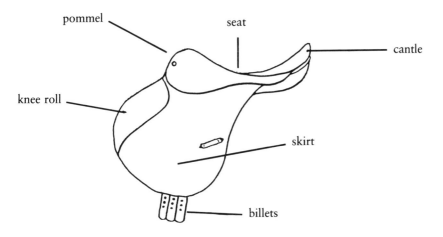

pommel

seat

cantle

knee roll

skirt

billets

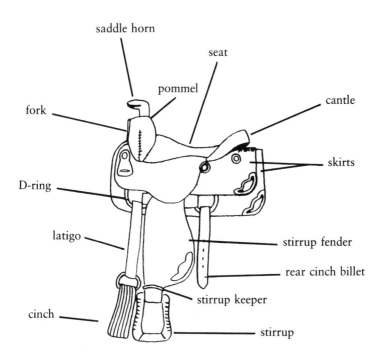

saddle horn

seat

pommel

cantle

fork

skirts

D-ring

latigo

stirrup fender

rear cinch billet

stirrup keeper

cinch

stirrup

seat. The seat may measure anywhere from 14 to 21 inches long from the back of the upper pommel to the middle of the cantle. It may have a solid pommel or a cut-back pommel for higher-withered horses. Attached to the seat are fully adjoined side skirts.

English saddles, usually lighter in weight than their Western counterparts, are attached to the horse by means of a girth that is run around and under the horse's barrel. Both ends of the girth are buckled onto billets, or straps, that are securely attached to the saddle. Metal stirrups hang from the side of the saddle by means of stirrup leathers, which are strong, supple leather straps. The outer parts of English saddles are usually made of leather, but in recent years synthetic materials have begun to be used in inexpensive saddles.

Dressage saddles generally have a deep, or very concave, seat and long side skirts that extend straight down on the barrel of the horse. This

Dressage saddle.

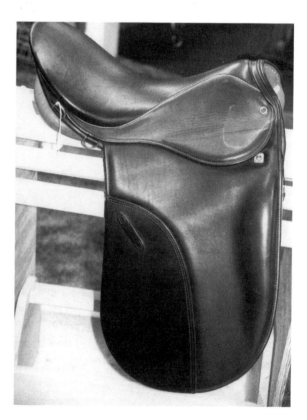

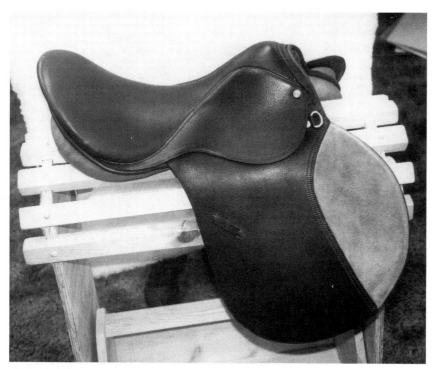

Hunt (or forward seat) saddle.

design enables the rider to sit deep in the saddle, in a relatively upright position with a long leg, and to be extraordinarily well balanced with the horse. Dressage riders use almost imperceptible seat and leg aids to communicate with the horse. For this reason, the saddle is designed to offer very close contact.

Hunt seat, or forward seat, saddles have either deep or shallow seats, depending on the rider's preference. The side skirts are not as long as those of dressage saddles, and the front edge of the skirt panels come farther forward on the horse's shoulder. Under the front upper to middle portion of the skirts are knee rolls, or padding. The hunt seat rider, when jumping obstacles, raises his seat up and out of the saddle and leans his body far forward. He uses his lower legs and knees to hold this position (called the half seat) on the horse. The more forward placement of the side skirts and the knee rolls offers security for the rider in this position.

Saddle seat saddles are lightweight, with very shallow seats and wide skirts. They distribute more of the rider's weight over the horse's

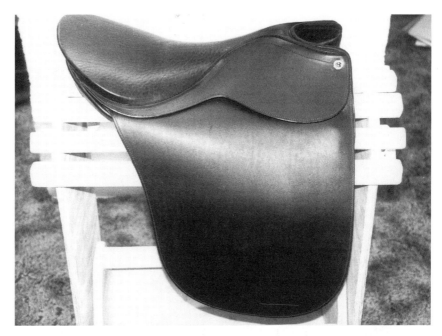

Saddle seat saddle.

*All-purpose English
saddle.*

haunches, thus lightening up the animal's front end and allowing his front legs great freedom of motion. This saddle design allows the horse to exhibit flashy front-end movement, a most desirable trait in saddle seat show classes.

All-purpose saddles usually have a medium-deep seat, moderately long and slightly forward side skirts and an unobtrusive knee roll. A well-designed all-purpose saddle offers comfort and security regardless of the activity, whether it be training or dressage practice, jumping over obstacles or simply enjoying a leisurely hack.

English saddles used to be placed directly on the horse's back, but today a saddle pad is used. The fleece not only offers more protection for the horse's back, but it also absorbs the horse's sweat. It should fit under every part of the saddle, including the side skirts. English saddle pads are usually made from man-made or natural fleece or wool felt; they often are manufactured to conform exactly to the shape of an individual saddle. Saddle seat saddles are still ridden without benefit of padding.

***

Bridles

When riding English style, you will use an English-style bridle. The English bridle consists of the crown piece, browband, cheek piece, cavesson, throatlatch, bit and curb chain. The "head straps" attach the bridle to the horse and the bridle equipment to the bridle. (The use of the bit and curb chain is explained in detail later on.) The cavesson goes around the horse's nose and encourages the horse to keep his mouth closed around the bit. Reins give the rider control and communication. The throatlatch keeps the bridle from slipping off the horse's head.

There are several kinds of English bridles, including the simple snaffle bridle, the pelham bridle, the full or double bridle and the mullen-mouth bridle. The bridle's name, and action, are derived from the type of mouthpiece, or bit, attached (i.e., the snaffle, curb or Mullen-mouth bit).

Originally, a snaffle bit was any bit with jointed or hinged parts. These joints could be located either in the mouthpiece or on the edges, or shanks, of the bit. The term is now commonly used to refer to a two-piece metal bit jointed together at the middle. Some such snaffle bits incorporate a middle section, making three-piece bits. The snaffle bit works as a directional aid at the corner of the horse's mouth and aids in collecting a horse through resistance on the bars and tongue of the horse. (The bars are the smooth area of the horse's mouth where there is a natural gap in the teeth, and across which the bit lays.) The simple snaffle bit works with little leverage and is, therefore, very mild. Very thin snaffles, or those made of twisted wire, are more severe and should be used rarely, and then only by a competent professional horse trainer.

The pelham bridle carries a curb bit, or a one-piece metal bar bit with a half-circle curve, or port, at the center. This port serves to relieve pressure on the horse's tongue and, with the aid of the curb chain under the horse's jaw, exerts pressure on the roof of the horse's mouth. All in all, the pelham bridle exerts leveraged pressure on the horse's tongue and bars, on the roof and corners of the mouth, under the chin, and at the sensitive poll. While this bridle offers a sensitive, experienced rider with good hands excellent communication and control, it can be quite harsh, even brutal, in the wrong hands. The severity of this bridle depends upon the fit of the bit to the horse's mouth, how tightly the curb chain is adjusted, upon the shape of the mouthpiece and upon the sensitivity of the rider's hands.

A double, or full, bridle is one that incorporates both a snaffle (or bridoon) and a curb bit, with a separate set of reins for each. The snaffle reins are used to indicate direction, and the curb reins are used to control impulsion. A full bridle is required in saddle seat show ring classes. It offers a high degree of control for the experienced horseman but should not be used by a novice rider nor on any horse not specifically trained to its use.

The mullen-mouth bit consists of a heavy, straight metal bar that lies across the bars and tongue of the horse's mouth. There is no curve in the middle of the mouthpiece, so when the reins are pulled, a considerable amount of pressure is exerted on the horse's tongue. This bit can be very severe, and its use should be limited to riders with good, experienced hands.

WESTERN RIDING

Saddles

English riding is considered the more classic form of horsemanship, and many instructors prefer to teach it, but many everyday horsemen prefer riding Western-style saddles. I recommend trying this style of riding before making any final decisions about tack.

Older-style Western saddles were extremely heavy, offered the rider poor contact with the horse and were built in a way that made good riding balance difficult. These shortcomings have been remedied, however, and many of today's Western saddles offer good contact and excellent balance. In comparison with English saddles they have some advantages—physical as well as psychological—in terms of rider security.

Western saddles have a high cantle and a horn on top of the pommel. The high-back cantle helps hold the rider in place while the horn, intended originally to fasten the rope used when roping cows, can be held onto by a novice rider when Fear or Insecurity rear their ugly heads. The seat of the Western saddle sits just above one or two leather skirts. Behind the seat, there are usually several long leather ties fastened to the skirts; the ties are for securing saddle bags, blanket rolls and other riding necessities. Although there is an infinite variety of Western stirrup shapes and styles, stirrups are commonly constructed of leather-wrapped wood and are hung by means of wide stirrup leathers attached to permanently affixed leather fenders. Metal rings are secured to the tree or the skirting, on both sides, at the side front and/or side rear of the saddle. From these rings hang leather latigos—wide, strong and extremely flexible leather straps used to attach the front cinch. The cinch, usually made of nylon webbing or heavy cotton cords, holds the saddle on the horse; nylon web cinches are usually lined with fleece. An additional rear girth strap may be attached to the rear metal rings.

There are many kinds of Western saddles, each designed for a particular job (e.g., reining, cutting, roping). Roping saddles have a relatively low cantle and a wooden saddle tree, which makes them large and heavy. The greater size and weight are necessary because such a saddle must bear enormous strain when a full-sized steer is being roped off it. The low cantle enables the roper to dismount quickly when he leaps off his horse to wrestle down a calf or steer.

Racing, or barrel racing, saddles are built with fiberglass trees and are lightweight. They are often made with just one skirt, which is cut short and round, rather than long and square. This design not only eliminates extra material and weight; it also allows the horse greater flexibility for bending around tight curves.

The more common Western saddles are pleasure and stock saddles, which are made for show, for everyday ranch work and for general-purpose riding. Often built on a fiberglass tree, they are frequently lightweight, well balanced and easy to ride. Seat sizes commonly vary from

Western stock saddle.

All-purpose Western saddle.

Ornately silvered Western show saddle and matching breast collar.

14 to 18 inches, measuring from the rear of the pommel to the center of the cantle. Seat size is chosen according to the size and weight of the rider. The fork, or space just over the horse's withers and under the pommel and saddle horn, may be designed high or low. Pleasure saddles may be made of plain, untooled leather or be very ornate, with silver appointments and intricate tooling.

Western saddle blankets are usually heavier than their English counterparts. Two or three blankets or pads may be used at one time. A horse with especially high withers may need a split saddle blanket. This blanket has a slot cut out at the front middle section, giving the withers more room for clearance under the pommel.

There are a number of other kinds of saddles that fit neither in the English or Western category. Perhaps the most notable of these is the Australian stock saddle. Although based on English design, these saddles are now permitted in many Western horse show classes. One characteristic that sets these saddles apart from any other style is the knee poly that is built into the saddle skirt, positioned just in front of the upper thigh. Since a knee can be braced against the poly, it offers extra security for a rider going downhill over rough terrain. Also the cantle is higher than in the typical English saddle.

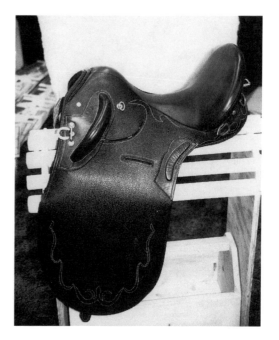

Australian stock saddle. Note the knee poly, which serves as an anchor for the thigh and knee when the rider is traveling downhill or over rough terrain.

Western Bridles

Since most horses trained Western-style are taught to neck rein rather than rely on direct mouth pressure for directional control, Western bridles usually carry curb bits, though one style, commonly called a Tom Thumb, has a snaffle mouthpiece. Western bits have metal shanks extending down both sides. Reins are attached at the end of these shanks, and leather curb straps are positioned under the chin. The severity of the bridle depends upon the fit, weight, thickness and style of the bit, the length of the shanks (the longer the shanks, the greater the leverage and severity), the tightness of the curb strap and the sensitivity of the rider's hands.

Some Western bridles, such as the mechanical hackamore and the bosal, are bitless. The bosal is commonly used as a training bridle. It produces action by means of a soft band over the nose and by pressure at the poll. The bosal can be extremely gentle on the young horse, and it can also offer an appreciable amount of restraint and control should the need arise. It does not, however, offer the subtle control needed to produce a finished horse.

Contrary to popular belief, mechanical hackamore bridles exert highly leveraged pressure on the bridge of the horse's nose, under the jaw and at the poll, and can be quite severe. A rider should be properly instructed in their use and action before riding a horse so equipped.

Many Western-trained horses are ridden on a loose rein. This is perhaps a good idea for a beginning rider, though care should be taken that the reins are not too forcefully snatched up when the horse is commanded to stop or reduce speed. Once the rider has learned to balance without benefit of reins, the horse can be ridden with light to moderate mouth contact.

FITTING TACK

What must be understood, regardless of the type of saddle you buy or the kind of riding you plan to do, is that the saddle must properly fit the horse and the rider.

When a saddle is set on the horse's back, with the pommel at the

Fork of the saddle. For proper saddle fit, the fork should fit so there is at least two fingers' width of clearance over the horse's withers when a rider is fully seated in the saddle.

midpoint over the withers, check to see that no part of the front edge of the saddle tree sits right over the back edge of your horse's front shoulder blade—a common saddle fitting error that restricts movement and hurts the horse. To understand how this affects a horse, ask a friend to hold a hard object, such as a board, right over one of your shoulder blades. Now make exaggerated swimming motions with that object held firmly in place. As uncomfortable as this is, think how much worse it would be if there was a 100-plus pound weight attached, such as there

Whether English or Western, the two most common types of bits are snaffle (top) and curb (bottom). Both bits are placed over, and work on, the bars and the tongue of the horse's mouth (left illustrations). Either style of bit should fit so there is about ½" clearance on either side of the horse's lips, and the lip should be pulled back so there is one wrinkle at the corner. The snaffle bit gives directional aid at the corner of the horse's mouth. The half-moon-shaped area of curb bit raises up and works on the roof of the horse's mouth when the reins are pulled back. The curb strap also exerts pressure under the horse's chin and up through the bridle straps to the sensitive poll. The long shanks on many styles of curbs give greater leverage, making the action more severe.

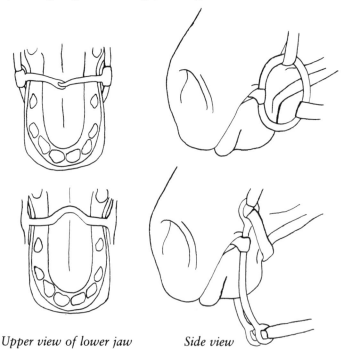

Upper view of lower jaw   *Side view*

is when your horse carries a rider. Be certain the animal's shoulder blade has ample room to move freely under saddle.

The fork of the saddle should clear the withers by two fingers' width, with the rider seated in the saddle. The saddle tree mustn't be too narrow if the horse is wide, or too wide if the horse is narrow-bodied. If he has a short back, make certain the back edge of the saddle doesn't restrict his hip movement. On a small horse, a saddle that's too big will restrict bending; a small saddle on a big horse will pinch. The center underside channel of an English saddle mustn't flatten out under the rider's weight. The bottom of the saddle should closely conform to the shape of your horse's back.

Once you're satisfied that the saddle fits the horse, make certain the rider fits the saddle. When the rider is seated, there should be about two fingers' width between his front upper thigh and the pommel of the saddle. On a Western saddle, the rider should be able to slide a hand sideways between his buttocks and the cantle. The stirrups should fall straight down from below the deepest part of the seat, so the rider's feet, when the legs are relaxed straight down, easily slip into the stirrups. Above all, the saddle must feel *comfortable*.

WHERE TO BUY TACK

There are any number of places to purchase good-quality new and used equipment: in tack shops, at horse and tack auctions and through classified and catalog advertising. You might purchase tack from friends and acquaintances. Often these avenues offer great savings. But you must be conscientious about putting your horse's well-being ahead of financial considerations.

Auctions give no opportunity for checking the fit between your horse and the saddle, and no opportunity for exchange or refund. So unless you have a very good idea of what kind and shape of saddle your horse requires (and eyeball fitting takes a great deal of talent and experience), purchasing saddles at auction is risky. Checking out saddles in classified ads is fine, but ask to try the saddle on the horse before final purchase. The same goes for tack shops; some reputable stores offer the buyer an opportunity to return the merchandise if it's not suitable. If you shop by mail and an item proves unacceptable, be aware that returning it may be time-consuming and inconvenient. If you purchase by mail

Tack shops provide great variety of choice, often offering both new and used merchandise. Many reputable shops allow for return of tack (in good condition) if it doesn't fit the horse.

order, choose well-established companies with good reputations.

The best way to fit a saddle to your horse and yourself is by contracting an experienced, reputable saddle maker to build a custom saddle for you. Such craftsmen advertise in local and national horse publications, or you may hear of one through word of mouth. One saddle maker where I live will build a well-constructed custom saddle for as little as $1,500. But costs may run several times this amount, depending on the kind of saddle required and the person contracted to do the work. Not every rider can afford such an item—but, if you can, it's a great long-term investment in your horsemanship. If you decide to investigate this route, ask the saddle maker for the names and addresses of past customers, and contact those people to make certain the saddle maker's work has been satisfactory. Arrange to see his handiwork.

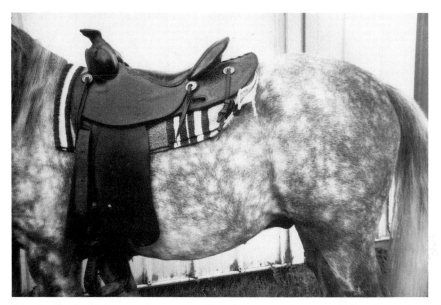

Handcrafted saddles can be an excellent long-term investment for the serious rider. This handmade saddle is more than twenty years old and is used hard (by a horse trainer) every day. The initial cost of such a saddle is more than offset by its long life, comfort and superior performance.

TIE-DOWNS, MARTINGALES, DRAW REINS

Tie-downs, standing martingales, draw reins and running martingales are tack devices used to position the horse's head. Tie-downs (Western) and standing martingales (English) are used to help keep the horse from tossing and throwing his head too high in the air. Head tossing, however, is too often a result of overbitting the horse and/or of poor hands.

A horse that is going to bolt will throw his head in the air, stiffen his neck and run. A tie-down or standing martingale may help prevent this but should be used only until other retraining methods (see Chapter Twelve) take effect. A horse that is continually ridden in these devices never unlearns his bad habits and may learn new evasive tactics to compensate for the restrictive equipment. And never count on such a device to control a horse that tends to rear. A tie-down will not prevent rearing but may cause a rearing animal to flip over backward. Don't ever

Western tie-down.

Tie-down prevents a gaming horse from flinging his head too high in the air as he rounds poles, increasing rider control.

let this happen to you. For safety's sake, stay off rearing horses altogether.

Draw reins (Western) and running martingales (English) are a different matter. These attach to the girth or saddle rings and run through the bit rings (draw reins) or the reins (standing martingale). Both devices teach the horse how to properly use his neck and poll, and how to hold his head. These can help to make a horse more responsive and give him an extremely attractive head set.

Draw reins and running martingales are very useful for the final, polishing phase of training, when a trainer is producing a finished horse. Running martingales, frequently used on jumping horses, must be carefully adjusted and appropriately used. The effect on the horse of all such training tools must be thoroughly understood by the handler before they are placed on a horse. They should never be used as a shortcut to more appropriate training.

Eight
FEEDING

*H*orses are grazing animals. Their digestive systems are designed to process small amounts of bulky, low-calorie feedstuff that move through their systems nearly full-time. By nature wild horses are not intended to do much more work than what is required to meander from one grazing spot to another, so a low-energy ration is sufficient for the wild horse.

Feeding domesticated horses in such a way would require either keeping them on good-quality, well-maintained pasture full-time, with little or no exercise, or else keeping them stall-bound and replenishing their mangers with hay every hour or so while offering a continuous source of fresh water. For most of us, neither choice is feasible. Once again we compromise between our needs and the horse's.

PROVIDING GOOD PASTURE

The best all-around and least-expensive horse feed you can provide is pasture forage. Good pasture forage for domestic horses is not an accident of nature but the result of careful planning and intelligent tending. First the soil should be tested, and any minerals lacking added to it; pastures frequently need to be limed, and often nitrogen is applied. Legumes (clovers, soybeans, lespedeza and alfalfa) are highly nutritious pasture plants that naturally increase the soil's nitrogen content.

Besides legumes, pastures usually contain a variety of pasture grasses. There's a wide variety of different grass seeds available— timothy, Bermudagrass, orchardgrass, fescue, bromegrass and Kentucky bluegrass. You will want to choose a tough, drought-resistant, self-propagating, highly nourishing and low-maintenance mixture of these

Good horse pasture like this takes intelligent planning. A fence through the center of the pasture allows for pasture rotation even on limited acreage.

grasses. The specific seed mixture you use will depend upon your soil and climate, what is already growing in your pasture area, how much acreage you have to cover, what tools you have to cover it with, your budget and how much time and equipment you can devote to maintenance. A commercial seed salesman or your county agricultural extension agent can provide soil analysis and information about the procedures and products most suited to your region and situation.

Pasture Problems

Once established, pastures require very little maintenance, *if* they are not allowed to become overgrown or overgrazed. Overgrown pasture plants provide more fiber and less nutrition than do younger plants. They also shade the ground so fewer young plants grow among them. Horses tend to snub such growth in favor of younger, tender, more succulent plants. This results in uneven grazing of the pasture, so some plant areas become overgrazed and weakened, while others become overgrown with plants that offer poor nutritional value.

Feeding hay from the ground, especially from overgrazed ground, may lead to heavy parasite infestation of horses.

This situation is to be avoided. It's also desirable to keep weeds to a minimum because they rob the soil of nutrition and eventually weaken and overtake good forage. A ten-acre pasture, if overgrazed and overgrown with weeds, may produce only as much good forage as one or two acres of well-tended land.

Parasitic infestation is another consideration. Parasites in horse droppings contaminate soil and grasses. It's necessary to eliminate these pasture pests as much as possible to prevent horses from becoming continually reinfested as they graze contaminated pasture.

Pasture Maintenance Routines

There are two measures you can take to prevent overgrown, overgrazed and weedy pastures and cut down on parasite infestation: Mow your pasture to keep it at an overall height of about four inches, and rotate your horses to a new pasture every three or four weeks. Mowing the pasture stunts the growth of broadleaf weeds, prevents all kinds of weeds from maturing and reseeding, keeps grasses to an optimal grazing length and exposes parasites to the sun, which destroys them. Rotating pastures prevents overgrazing, which weakens the plants. It also interrupts the life cycle of parasites, as these must be provided with a host animal in order to live and multiply. Take the host animal—your horse—out of the field for about a month and many kinds of parasites will simply die.

You can rotate pastures even if your acreage is limited. Simply run an electric wire through the pasture, cutting off access to part of it. Two to three acres of pasture will support a 1,000-pound horse year-round if it is regularly mowed and if half at a time is left to rest for four-week periods. If you have less pasture than this, plan to supplement your horse's diet with hay and/or grain; put him in the barn and corral for a couple of weeks every month or so to give the pasture a rest.

Managing Seasonal Variations in Forage

If you live in part of the country with dramatic seasonal variations, your pasture forage has different growth and nutritional qualities at different times of the year. It is most prolific, rich and high in water content during the spring growing season. For this reason, if you are switching your horse from winter's hay to grass pasture in the spring, do it gradually. Suddenly switching from dry hay to rich spring pasture may cause a horse to colic and/or founder. Limit first spring pasture forays to half an hour. Over about three weeks' time, you can gradually increase this to full-time grazing.

Summer grass is nutritious and fast growing, qualities that diminish as the year progresses. By late fall, there is very little nutritional value in most pasture forage, and plants are also growing so slowly that they can quickly be overgrazed. Even if you've faithfully mowed and rotated your pastures, you will now need to start supplementing your horse's diet with hay. If you live in a cold region, hay will make up the bulk of your horse's winter diet.

CHOOSING GOOD-QUALITY HAY

Though hay provides mostly bulk in your horse's diet, it can contribute substantially to his level of nutrition. On average, a horse requires about one and one-half pounds of hay per day for every 100 pounds of body weight, or about 15 pounds per day for a 1,000-pound animal.

Learn what to look for when purchasing hay, and choose carefully. Good-quality hay is much like good-quality pasture: It takes conscientious planning for optimum growth and high nutritional value. There are three kinds of hay: grain, grasses and legumes.

Grain hays include wheat and oat hays. If these are used, the dried plants should contain the grain kernels. Like other grain products, grain hays attract rodents. But, unlike other grain products, grain hay cannot be sealed up and protected from these pests. Because such hay is hard to keep properly, it is not commonly used.

Grasses make up the major portion of most hays, and are often mixed with legumes. Timothy grass with a 20 to 30 percent mix of clover is a very common type of hay. Hays made up of legumes only, such as clover or alfalfa, are too rich for horses, and may cause colic and/or founder.

Good-quality hay should be sweet-smelling, green in color, and have plenty of plant heads and flowers with few tough stems or obvious weeds. It should also appear clean and never moldy or dusty—this point cannot be overemphasized.

Horses' respiratory systems are especially sensitive to mold and dust. Horses that are especially sensitive can develop what is commonly called hay allergy, a condition that produces asthma-like symptoms, or "heaves." Because horses suffering from heaves have trouble expiring air, their flank muscles are "heaved" upward in an exaggerated effort to expel air from their lungs, a response that may be triggered by the breathing in of particles of dust or mold from hay.

One remedy for this situation is to wet down the hay of any horse known to suffer from this condition. Another solution is to forgo hay feeding altogether and offer such a horse pelleted feed. But by far the best way to handle this condition is to avoid triggering such a sensitivity altogether: Never, but *never,* offer your horse dusty or moldy hay. Don't even use it as bedding, or throw it where your horse can reach over the fence to snatch a bite or two. Besides contributing to respiratory disease, some hay molds can be fatally toxic.

After examining hay for purchase but before laying out any cash, there are two steps you should take. Ask for a sample bale of hay to try out on your horse. Horses, like people, possess different tastes. What is palatable to one may taste obnoxious to another. Then, to guarantee its nutritional value, take a jarful of your intended purchase to your county agricultural agency or local feedstore for analysis. Such an analysis can tell you whether the hay you plan to purchase is low in an important trace element called selenium (which means you will also need to purchase selenium supplements, or high-selenium grain) and whether the product tests acceptably high in other basic nutrients.

Storing Hay

The way hay is stored will affect quality. It should be stored out of the sunlight, which destroys nutrition. Bales should be staggered so they're not stacked too tightly together, to facilitate any drying that still needs to be done. Hay that is too wet when baled and/or that is baled and stored too tightly will develop mold. It may even become a source of spontaneous combustion.

To check for proper drying of baled hay, slide your hand into the center of a bale. It should feel only slightly warm. If it feels hot, the twine must be cut and the hay spread out somewhere—either in your loft or outdoors under the protection of a tarpaulin—to air dry. This may seem like a tremendous bother, but it's not nearly so bothersome as losing your barn and livestock to fire or as losing the use of a good horse to heaves.

The big, round bales of hay that have become common sights on the fields of farms over the past several years aren't practical for most horse owners. First, they require a specially equipped tractor for handling. Second, if they are kept in the field, as is common practice, the natural elements—rain, wind, sun—rob the top layers of hay of nutrition while rodents infest the deeper layers. As is often the case, new isn't necessarily improved, and bigger isn't better. Stick to small bales, if you can.

Paying for Hay

The price you pay for hay can vary widely depending on the growing year local farmers have had, the distance the hay has to be transported and the profit the farmer intends to make. Sometimes you can arrange to exchange haying or other farm labor for hay. If you do this, be sure you've researched the wage this kind of work normally brings and the standard cash price of the hay, so you get a fair exchange. Besides saving money, many horsemen enjoy the outdoor labor of haying.

If you own enough land and enjoy outdoor labor, you might consider putting in your own hay. This is easy to do if you own enough pasture to segment it into three or more sections. As your horse or horses graze one section, you can be mowing, drying and baling hay from another section, while yet a third segment rests. Pasture that has been grazed must be raked to aid in the breakdown and elimination of droppings, and be given several weeks to recover from grazing before being hayed. Leave four inches of height when mowing.

You need to mow, in any case. If you've gone to the trouble of planting good forage, why not put the mowed forage to good use? If you don't own haying equipment, you may be able to work out a rental or labor trade agreement with a local farmer or another horseman.

GRAIN TYPES AND USES

A horse's energy, or food, requirements vary according to his natural metabolic rate and his workload. An animal that does little more than stand in a pasture or box stall should do well on just pasture and hay. But a horse put to regular, heavy use, or one that is growing, pregnant or training hard, even one with a food-burning metabolism set on high, will require more. Both hay and pasture are high-bulk, low-energy foods. Because the horse's digestion system can accommodate only a limited amount of food at any time, an animal with greater caloric requirements requires a high-energy, more nutritionally concentrated source of food. This source is best found in grains.

Corn, oats, barley, rye, wheat and milo are all used in horse-grain mixtures, though not all mixtures contain all of these elements. Horse grains are generally more expensive per hundred weight than other types of livestock feed. But other livestocks' nutritional needs are far different from those of the horse. Although purchasing cattle grain, for example, might seem to be a good way to cut expenses, you won't be getting good nutritional value for your money. Be sure to purchase a grain mixture specially formulated for horses.

Unless your horse has special nutritional needs, the grain mixture you choose should not be higher than 11 to 12 percent protein. This level meets the needs of all but the hardest-working or fastest-growing animal. With more protein than this, your horse's system may be distressed, especially if he is an older animal. Most commercial horse feeds are sweetened, usually with molasses, making the food more palatable, which is good so long as it isn't done to excess.

Commercially processed horse feeds may consist of whole grains, cracked grains and pellets or a variety of finely milled grains. Different horses thrive on different types and mixtures. Often older horses do better on finely milled grains, as their teeth and digestion aren't as efficient as a young animal's. Other horses turn their noses up at anything but whole grains and pellets. By all means, experiment to see what works best. But, as you experiment, be sure not to switch grain mixtures too quickly.

A horse's digestive system needs time to adjust to different feedstuffs. Failure to allow enough time may result in colic. When you switch grain products, mix the new grain with the old at a ratio of 25/75 for a day or two. Increase the amount of new grain over several days until it has replaced the old. Then give the new product time to work; use the new grain mixture for six weeks before deciding whether it's meeting your horse's nutritional needs.

How Much of a Good Thing?

How can you tell how much grain to feed your horse? No matter what sort of formula you're given, the truth is that feeding is largely a matter of gaining experience through trial and error. Does the animal seem a bit thin and lethargic, though he's been dewormed and is otherwise in good health? Then add to his rations, a quarter-can or half-can scoop at a time (see next section). Has he become abnormally hot tempered or seem too full of energy? Is he getting a crested neck and sort of fat-looking? Perhaps he's getting too much feed for his work load. Find out by cutting back and observing the animal's response.

Only experience with your horse will teach you his particular nutritional needs, and these will change from time to time according to the season, the use he's put to and his age. Get in the habit of evaluating your horse's condition regularly, and be prepared to adjust his feed accordingly.

Establishing Weight by Volume

You may have heard horses should be fed by weight rather than volume. This is true, but realistically, few of us weigh out our animals' feed every morning and evening. Instead, we usually measure out their rations in so many scoops or partial scoops to a feeding. But you can do this and still have a good idea how much feed, by weight, your horse is using. Once you've settled on a grain product, screw a handle onto a one-pound coffee can, and use this can as a scoop. Weigh the scoop when it is full, three-quarters, one-half, and one-quarter full (the circular indentations on the can make this easy). Now mark the weight by volume at each of these points. If your horse seems to need a decrease or increase in feed, simply use these markings to fine-tune his rations, one-quarter can at a time. This way you eliminate the need to weigh feed every time a change in amount is called for, yet you have a good idea of how much grain he's eating, by weight. Be sure, however, to reweigh grains if you switch products, as there will be a wide difference in the volume-to-weight ratio among different types and brands of horse grains.

Proper storage of hay and grain protects feed quality. A covered grain bin prevents horses from accidentally over-ingesting rich feed, which may cause colic and/or founder.

Storing Grain

It's important that grain be stored in a sealed, rodent-proof container. It also should be "horse-proofed," that is, stored separately from the stall area of the barn and preferably behind locked doors. If a horse accidentally gains access to grain products, he will overeat. Since overingestion of grain leads to serious colic or founder or both, a horse may literally eat himself to death. You never want to have the experience of going out to the barn to discover your horse munching contentedly out of a carelessly secured grain bin. A little extra caution when planning your grain storage can prevent a real tragedy.

Nine

HEALTH CARE

*F*ew things are as distressing to the horseman as discovering that his horse has come up lame or ill. Horses are vulnerable to many health risks. Fortunately, proper management will significantly reduce those risks, allowing an animal to remain disease and injury free for many years.

THE HEALTHY HORSE

One of the first things you can do to ensure your horse's well-being is to purchase an animal in good health. This may seem obvious, but too often enthusiasm and unwillingness to pay for a vet's services overwhelm prudence, and a horse is purchased without being checked by a vet. Don't make this mistake. Take the time to have a veterinarian of *your* choice—not the seller's—give your prospective purchase a thorough examination. As a number of chronic diseases and lamenesses can be detected only by a veterinarian, this precaution may ultimately save you thousands of dollars and many hours of heartache.

It's not uncommon for a compassionate horse lover to purchase an ill or poorly kept animal out of pity, expecting to bring it around through good nourishment, veterinary care and plenty of love. This is commendable, but don't do it unless you're prepared to assume the loss of a horse.

A friend of mine purchased a thin, ill-kept Saddlebred mare from a local equine rescue group. This mare was her daughter's first 4-H horse, and they invested all the money they could afford in her purchase and health care. It seemed to be a match made in heaven. Within a week after the family acquired her, the mare was following the little girl around like a lovesick puppy. She was perfectly obedient under saddle, and as her weight increased she bloomed into a lovely horse.

Then one night about two months later the mare colicked. The vet came by several times and did all he could, but he warned the owners that the case seemed hopeless. By late afternoon the next day, the horse was dead. The little girl was inconsolable. Her mother, having spent so much money on the mare, couldn't afford another horse. This mare's fatal colic almost surely resulted from the overload of parasites she'd carried before she was purchased by this family. Because of earlier neglect, her intestines were irreparably damaged.

This sad story demonstrates just one way neglected horses are poor health risks. There are usually plenty of healthy animals available who need good homes just as badly as their more unfortunate relatives. Purchasing a healthy horse that needs a good home and preventing it from suffering a similar sad fate is a good deed, and one you can do without shouldering unacceptably high risk.

PARASITES

Assuming you've purchased a healthy horse, there are a few things you must do to keep him that way. Start by instituting a regular deworming program. Parasites are a real danger to the health of a horse, and, as the story above illustrates, they may even contribute to a horse's death. All horses carry internal parasites; some are relatively harmless, while others do a great deal of internal damage.

Grazing horses usually contract parasites when they ingest immature worm larvae, or eggs. The larvae migrate through the horse's digestive tract to the intestinal area, where they settle, feed, mature—and multiply. When the animal excretes droppings, newly laid larvae are deposited onto the ground, where they lie in wait until an unsuspecting grazing animal ingests them and the cycle is repeated.

Horses may be infested by millions of worms. Those carrying a heavy parasite load do not receive proper nourishment from their food. They become weak, lethargic, anemic and prone to illness and disease. Young horses may have their growth stunted. The internal damage done to intestines and the walls of arteries by strongyles, in particular, can result in serious colic, impaction, gangrenous tissue in the intestine or rupture of the blood vessels supplying the intestines. Any of these conditions can prove fatal.

Rotating and mowing pastures help keep parasites at bay by exposing the ground to sunlight, which kills most parasite eggs. The life cycle of parasites depends upon a host animal ingesting the eggs within four or five weeks of the time they're deposited on the ground. If a horse is kept out of a pasture long enough, the larvae in that pasture will die. It is also not a good practice to feed your horses hay from the stall floor or ground, as doing so increases parasite ingestion.

If your horse is turned out to pasture, check him regularly for bot eggs. A botfly is a large fly that somewhat resembles a bee. Botflies deposit small, yellow eggs directly onto the horse's hair shafts during the summer. These eggs are literally "glued on," usually around the front legs, shoulders and neck. They cause the horse to itch; as he licks or bites himself to combat the itch, the bot eggs get into his mouth and he becomes internally infected. The only good way to handle botfly eggs is by scraping them off the horse with a special, rough bot-fly utensil or with the edge of a dull knife.

Despite all precautions, parasites will find a way to survive, so horses must be dewormed regularly. Deworming used to be a complicated and risky procedure, in which veterinarians administered dangerously high dosages of drugs through tubes threaded through the horse's nose into his stomach. But no more. There are now a variety of owner-administered paste dewormers to choose from.

Most deworming products are effective against particular types of parasites. The repeated use of any one type of deworming drug eventually desensitizes the affected parasite families to the dewormer's main chemical component; in other words, most dewormers become less and less effective with repeated use. We combat this tendency by rotating paste dewormers, treating the horse with one type of dewormer one time and using another brand the next.

Recently products containing ivermectin, a broad-spectrum parasiticide, have become available. Ivermectin products are effective against a great variety of parasites, and so far have not produced widespread resistance. They can be used regularly without losing their effectiveness. However, because ivermectin products are relatively expensive, you may still decide to rotate, using an ivermectin dewormer one time and a less expensive product the next.

Horses kept in warm climates must be dewormed about every eight weeks. Those living in colder regions require the same schedule, except during the coldest winter months. Because a hard frost kills parasite eggs, your last deworming of the year can be done one month after the first hard frost, and your next deworming session can wait until four weeks after the first spring thaw. Use a broad-spectrum product for the last deworming of the season, as you'll want to be certain your horse is relatively free of parasites through the winter. Whatever products you use, be sure to follow all package directions carefully. Though common, deworming products are potent drugs that should be used with caution.

EXTERNAL PARASITES

Horses are also prone to external parasites. These make the animal miserable and contribute to the spread of disease. Common external pests include several varieties of flies, mosquitos, bees, ticks, lice and mange mites.

In warm months, stable your horse during the hours of the day when flies and mosquitos are most active. If your horse's skin is especially sensitive to biting insects, you may need to keep a light sheet on him and/or apply insect repellant as further protection. If face flies are a persistent problem, purchase a special face net or a whisk that attaches to the horse's halter and swishes insects away as he moves.

Once or twice a week, gently swab out the horse's ears with clear, warm water. Carefully dry the ear. Apply a thin layer of petroleum jelly inside the ear, being careful not to probe too deeply. This procedure prevents small insects from using your horse's sensitive ears as an eating and breeding ground.

Don't neglect regular grooming, paying particular attention to the underline of the belly, the anus and the pastern areas, as these sites commonly harbor parasites. Scrape off all botfly eggs as they appear. Keep any open wounds on your horse meticulously clean, and protect them with bandaging and/or medication. Some external parasites attack the tissues of open wounds causing infection and, often serious damage.

Lice and ticks require specific treatment. You should suspect that your horse is infested with these if he rubs continually on stall walls or corral fencing, if he becomes rough-coated or develops bald spots or if he becomes unusually cranky and starts biting and scratching his flanks and belly.

Lice are contagious and easily contracted from another infected horse, or through shared blankets, cinches or grooming equipment—one good reason why sharing equipment is a poor idea. Horse lice will not, however, attach to human beings. As a rule, lice become evident during the winter or spring months, when the horse sports a long, shaggy and—to the louse, at least—inviting coat of hair.

Ticks, picked up in the woods or pasture, are not contagious. The recent spread of Lyme disease warrants especially good grooming following every trail ride in areas where the tiny deer tick is known to habitate. If you trail ride, contact your local agricultural extension agency to inquire about the risk in your region, and to learn how to protect both human and horse against these parasites.

Lice and ticks can be detected by scraping your fingernails along the bottom of the horse's jaw, between the jawbones. Catch the debris that falls from this area on a white sheet of paper, and examine it under a magnifying glass. If your horse has lice, you'll find small (1/8- to 1/4-inch-long) red or brown cigar-shaped insects on your hand. Ticks are round and, if distended with blood, may be as large as one inch across.

If you discover ticks or lice, dust or spray your horse with an insecticide approved for the treatment of these parasites. Since lice eggs will survive and hatch following dusting, the treatment must be repeated in about a week. You'll need to treat any other horses, blankets and equipment that may be a source of reinfestation. Follow product directions.

If external skin problems persist, despite treatment, then suspect mange mites, and call your veterinarian for diagnosis and treatment.

IMMUNIZATIONS

Good health maintenance dictates that your horse receive regular immunizations. Horses are especially vulnerable to tetanus, a paralyzing disease caused by a bacterium called *Clostridium tetani*. This extremely widespread bacterium lives in most soils. Horses are also highly susceptible to two common contagious viral diseases, rhinopneumonitis and equine influenza. You should immunize your horse against all three of these diseases every twelve months. Your veterinarian might also recommend inoculating against Potomac horse fever, botulism, strangles and the eastern, western, and Venezuelan strains of encephalomyelitis. Depend on your veterinarian to suggest and provide appropriate inoculations. Immunization needs vary according to the region of the country you live in, the conditions under which you keep your horse, whether or not a mare is in foal and the viruses that are currently making the rounds.

EQUINE INFECTIOUS ANEMIA (SWAMP FEVER)

Equine infectious anemia (EIA), or swamp fever, is a viral disease that affects only horses, mules and donkeys. No cure is currently available for animals with swamp fever, and the disease may be either active, chronic or inactive within the animal's system. The problem is that, though inactive EIA can be undetectable, some horses are carriers of the disease; though free of symptoms themselves, they can still infect other horses, which may succumb to the disease. For this reason most states and all major race tracks and horse shows require horses to be regularly tested for EIA.

Coggins Test

A blood test called the Coggins test will determine whether or not a horse carries the EIA virus. A veterinarian must draw the blood sample and prepare the necessary paperwork to formally establish a horse's status. The horse's blood is sent to a lab and tested. If it tests negative (as do 99 1/2 percent of all horses), you will receive dated Coggins papers to that effect. If, however, the animal tests positive, it must either be humanely put down or kept in permanent quarantine, completely isolated from other equines for the rest of its life.

Since the Coggins test is required under so many different circumstances, check with your veterinarian to determine how frequently blood should be taken in your area and then keep the testing on your horse up to date. If you plan to show your horse, contact show officials well in advance to inquire about their specific EIA policy; many shows require a negative Coggins test within 15 to 60 days of the animal arriving at the show grounds.

FOOT CARE

Even when your horse is well kept and fed, regularly dewormed, deloused, tested and inoculated against all manner of disease, there's still another good maintenance practice a conscientious horse lover will not overlook: regular foot care.

No foot, no horse. The horse's foot is a marvel of engineering and, were he kept in his wild state, would require no attention. But we demand that our horses carry extra weight, work on hard surfaces, jump over high obstacles and stand for hours in dry pastures and filthy stalls where their hoof walls are subject to debilitating conditions of every description. It's essential that we provide the extra protection needed for healthy foot maintenance under these unnatural conditions.

Accustom your horse to regular foot care by cleaning his feet at least three times weekly, and every time you put him to use. If the frog of his foot becomes soft and oozes a black, foul-smelling substance, chances are he's contracted thrush, a bacterial disease affecting the frog of the foot. To combat this, keep his feet and stall area meticulously dry and clean, and treat the sole of his feet with a 7-percent iodine solution. If the problem persists for longer than three or four days, treat with Kopertox, straight bleach or a copper sulphate solution. The latter is made by mixing 1 1/2 cups of copper sulphate (purchased at your feed or agricultural supply store) with one gallon of water. Such products must touch nothing but the sole and frog of the foot, as they are caustic and may damage skin and burn the hair off the horse's hide.

Routine farrier work is a must. A farrier is a professional caretaker of horse's feet. He will trim your horse's feet to a length and angle appropriate for the animal's natural conformation, his use and his living conditions. He will also shoe your horse, using the right size shoe, and will custom shape the shoes for a good fit. A good farrier's work will result in eliminating common gait problems. Over time his work may improve the animal's natural way of going. What's more, the shoes he puts on will stay on for at least six weeks and, if one doesn't, the shoe will be reset free of charge. Although a good farrier uses little force, his manner and methods elicit respect from a horse. He'll set you up on a foot-care schedule appropriate to your horse's needs and will stick to that schedule, barring someone else's emergency. It's hard to say how to choose a good farrier. But, like true love, once you're fortunate enough to find one, you'll know it.

A good farrier works hard and is worth his weight in gold.

GETTING PROFESSIONAL HELP

The same can be said about searching for a good veterinarian. The work of both farrier and veterinarian is time-consuming and demanding, and requires a great deal of knowledge and technical skill. When you find farriers and vets whose work seems worthy of respect, cherish them. Pay their invoices promptly. Unless there's a true emergency, avoid requesting services at inopportune times, such as evenings or weekends. If a course of treatment is suggested, follow instructions carefully and carry the treatment through to the end. When you expect a service visit, have your groomed horse in a clean, dry and well-lit space. Accustom your horse to being handled all over, especially his feet. The professional horse-care person shouldn't have to train your horse or risk injury when handling him.

Establish a relationship with a reliable veterinarian before an emergency strikes. These men and women can't earn a decent livelihood by running from one emergency to another. Besides, their main business should be preventive health maintenance. Too often horse people purchase their dewormers and immunization products from a mail order supply company, thus depriving the local veterinarian a fairly earned profit. Then they expect the vet to jump out of bed and come running the first time a horse colics or runs into a fence. Use your veterinarian for routine work, and he'll get to know your horse. This will enable him to do a better job if an emergency arises. Routine professional health care will help avert some emergency situations altogether.

If you've enlisted the services of a good farrier, it won't be necessary to go into detail here about the various problems horses can have with their feet. Your farrier will enlighten you, as necessary. Neither will I need to tell you how to diagnose illness or care for a sick horse if you take my advice and develop a working relationship with a reliable veterinarian. However, there are some health-related and first-aid practices every horse owner should be familiar with, including conditions that require an immediate emergency call to the veterinarian.

LAMENESS

If you notice your horse has come up lame, first clean out all four feet with a hoof pick to make sure there are no stones or other foreign objects causing the problem. If you find nothing, you'll need to determine which foot or leg is bothering the horse and whether it is a supportive or swinging leg lameness. A supportive lameness is one that causes the horse pain when the leg is on the ground. With swinging leg lameness, the horse's natural movement is altered because of pain in his legs or body.

Ask another person to walk the horse across a level, stone-free surface and observe carefully. Does the horse avoid putting any weight on one leg, or wince or limp when a particular leg is placed on the ground? If the signs of pain aren't obvious, you have to look further. Ask the person helping you to trot the horse. Observe the animal from all angles—front, back and sides. Does his head bob up and down unevenly? If the lameness is supportive and affects a front limb, when the horse's affected foot hits the ground his head will rise; it will lower when his sound leg hits the ground. If the lameness originates in a hind leg, you'll note the pelvis on the affected side rising higher than on the sound side. As that side of the pelvis rises, the horse's head will lower. Such movements are the horse's effort to take weight off the painful limb.

If you can pinpoint the limb that is affected and you note no obvious injury or abnormal movement indicating a swinging leg injury, check the foot of that limb carefully. If you can see nothing out of order, thoroughly scrape the entire sole of the foot, using a sharp hoof knife, until the sole has a clean, white surface. Press the point of the knife hard into various parts of the sole to see if the horse will respond, indicating a tender spot. Then scrape further down in that spot, if you can. If you come upon blood specks, discolored areas or pus, continue scraping. You may find a nail or other object lodged in the foot, a hole where such an object gained entry or a place where infection has set in following an injury.

If you find an object embedded in the sole of the foot, remove it and scrape the sole out thoroughly in about a one-inch area around the hole. If pus, a hole, blood stains or other evidence of injury is evident, use your hoof knife to thoroughly clean and open up the area at and around the damage, to facilitate drainage of the infection. Then follow up by having your vet administer tetanus antitoxin and prescribe further treatment. Be sure to keep the sole of the foot clean of debris. Cleanliness can be maintained by using a special horse boot on the affected foot (available through your vet or at most tack or animal supply stores); or you can pack the sole of the foot with clean cotton rags, secured with duct tape. If your vet prescribes epsom salt soaks, rub hoof dressing regularly on the walls of the foot to help restore moisture.

A swinging leg injury or limitation is another matter, requiring different methods of diagnosis and treatment. Such an injury involves a joint and may originate anywhere from the shoulder or hip of the horse on down through the front or rear legs.

An ill-fitting saddle may hinder motion at the hip or shoulder, causing soreness or gait limitation. Whenever a horse is exhibiting gait problems that cannot be directly attributed to a supportive leg injury, this possibility should be investigated and the fit of your tack closely checked. Sometimes a stress injury or arthritis limits the motion of a leg or legs. A veterinarian can perform various flexion tests to pinpoint a problem and suggest appropriate treatment.

If it's apparent you're dealing with a serious swinging leg injury, if there's disfigurement of the leg, severe stiffness in any part of the body or a great deal of pain, call your veterinarian. If the lameness seems minor, you may choose to give the horse a day or two of stall rest.

Should the lameness be caused by a minor twist or contusion, this rest should be all the treatment necessary. If there's no improvement or if the lameness becomes more severe after a couple days' rest, then call your veterinarian. If neglected, minor lameness can quickly accelerate into a major problem.

Laminitis (Founder)

Laminitis, or founder, is a disease of the soft, sensitive laminae that bonds the foot to the hoof. Usually, but not often, laminitis affects the two front feet; it never affects only one foot. If neglected, this disease may result in the rotational displacement of the distal bone in the leg and eventually lead to dropped sole, which will permanently disable the horse.

The causes of laminitis are many, including overingestion of rich grain or spring grass, placenta retention after foaling, hard stress to the horse's feet, acute illness and hormonal imbalances. Feeding grain or watering a horse too soon after hard work may also trigger laminitis.

Whatever the cause, founder must be dealt with as quickly as possible. The horse suffering from laminitis may stand in an unnatural position, with his front feet camped out before him and/or his back feet pulled way in underneath him. He may lay down and be reluctant to move when standing up. When he does move, his gait may be stilted. Acute laminitis may be accompanied by shaking, sweating, elevated respiration and pulse rates. The feet may feel hot to the touch.

How to treat laminitis? If you suspect founder, stand the horse in cold water and call your veterinarian immediately.

OTHER HEALTH PROBLEMS

Bleeding

If you discover your horse is bleeding profusely, your first priority is to get the bleeding stopped. Take a clean cotton cloth, folded thick, and press it directly into the wound, as hard as you can. Hold the cloth tightly over the wound or bandage it tightly if the wound affects the legs, until the bleeding is stopped. If bleeding persists despite strong direct pressure, contact a veterinarian for emergency treatment. Until he arrives, continue to apply strong pressure directly to the wound in an effort to stem the flow of blood.

If your horse's nose is bleeding, it will probably stop on its own. If it should fail to do so within a half hour or so, if the bleeding is profuse or if nosebleeds become a chronic problem, contact your veterinarian.

Injuries and Wounds

Horses are prone to injury and wounds of all sorts. They may run into barbed wire, scrape a front leg with a back foot or fall down onto a sharp object. A dirty cinch may cause a nasty gall, while a low-pommeled saddle can rub a sore at the top of the withers. Treatment of a sore or wound depends on its type and severity. There is, however, one constant in the treatment of all but the most superficial wounds: open wounds require that the horse receive a tetanus vaccination.

Shallow surface scratches and abrasions on the horse's hide that do not cut deeply enough to affect muscle tissue can be cleaned with warm water. Apply a light coating of antibiotic spray, as well as an insect repellent if insects are a problem. Be vigilant during the healing process and make sure infection doesn't set in.

You can also treat puncture wounds, if they're not too large or deep. Soak a cotton swab with a 7 percent solution of iodine, and insert it into the wound. Carefully, but thoroughly, swab out the wound. Repeat this treatment each day, until the injury is healed. If it fails to heal, you should suspect the presence of a foreign object, such as wood chips or the rusted point of a piece of barbed wire. If you can't find any such foreign matter and the wound hasn't visibly started to heal in two to three days or if there's any sign of infection, such as swelling, redness or pus, call your veterinarian.

Saddle sores are open wounds caused by tack rubbing on the horse's hide; galls are infected saddle sores. Dirty blankets and cinches may be the cause of saddle sores, as can poorly fitted tack. Sores may result from an out-of-condition horse being used too hard, too fast. Sometimes a heavy, inept rider will bounce enough to cause the saddle to slide around, resulting in a sore.

After you've ridden your horse, check his saddle, withers and girth areas carefully. If you see any dry spots in an otherwise wet blanket area, be aware that this spot is under pressure. Keep a close watch on this spot. A tender, raised or swollen spot may be the precursor to an actual sore. These conditions call for extra rest for the horse, extra padding for the area when he's used and a gradual conditioning program. Saddles, cinches and blankets should fit well and be regularly cleaned.

If a saddle sore develops, rest the horse until it is healed. During that time, clean the sore with antibiotic soap, rinse, then apply an antibiotic ointment or spray to facilitate healing and prevent infection. If the sore becomes red, weepy and inflamed, then it has become a gall, or infected sore. Call your veterinarian. Don't ignore saddle sores, as they don't go away by themselves. Neglect may result in permanent, deep damage to the tissues.

Serious puncture wounds, injuries that tear into the muscle wall, those involving the eyelid, wounds that appear infected, and anything but the most minor damage to a leg definitely require the service of a professional. Until that person arrives, get bleeding under control, reassure and calm your horse and clean out the injured area by rinsing with an abundance of clear, lukewarm water. DO NOT apply powders or ointments, as these may hinder the veterinarian's ability to effectively suture the wound.

Eye Injury

On occasion your horse may come into the barn with a red, weepy eye, or even one swelled shut altogether. Check the affected eye with a penlight, looking first directly into the eye and then across the cornea (the clear lens over the horse's eye) to see if you can detect any rips or tears to the cornea. If you see a rip or tear more than one-quarter inch in diameter, call your veterinarian *immediately*. If you fail to discover obvious damage, then it's possible the horse has suffered a slight scrape or has gotten a very small seed or other foreign object in his eye. Sometimes a foreign object has been washed out by the body's natural tearing mechanism, but the initial irritation has resulted in a slight infection or inflammation called conjunctivitis.

If the eye appears to have suffered only mild trauma or if you suspect a simple case of conjunctivitis, flush it well with clear lukewarm water three or four times a day. If a very slight scrape is visible on the cornea, treat it with an eye antibiotic containing *only* antibiotic and *no* cortisteroid. Inappropriate treatment of eye injuries with cortisteroid ointment may result in blindness. Keep the horse stabled and the light level as low as possible. If the eye has not healed in three or four days or if the problem at any time appears to be worsening, seek professional help.

Colic

Colic is a general term used to describe the acute distress exhibited by horses in pain; more specifically it refers to intestinal disturbances in the horse. According to sources in the equine insurance industry, colic is the leading cause of death of horses, accounting for one-third of all insurance death claims. It is estimated that one out of ten cases of colic results in death. If your horse is colicking, *call your veterinarian without delay.*

A horse with colic may bite, kick or paw at his flanks, stamp and paw the ground, sweat, lie down and thrash or simply stretch out on the ground. He may stand up and stretch out as though to urinate, grunt loudly or switch or pump his tail. Colicking horses are extremely restless, sometimes dangerously so. Avoid handling a colicking horse by yourself.

If you suspect colic, keep the animal comfortable until the vet arrives, and try to prevent him from going down to roll or thrash, which may cause a twisted bowel, a fatal complication. Horsemen are usually quick to suggest that a colicking horse be walked around, but don't overdo it. If ten minutes of walking doesn't help to relieve gas pressure and calm the horse, then an hour or two aren't likely to help either. Too much walking will merely wear out an already distressed animal.

Instead, watch your horse. If he appears to be only mildly uncomfortable, you may turn him out in an enclosed corral or pen. It's fine for him to lie down on the ground without rolling or thrashing around. If he does start to roll, get him up immediately. If your horse is in hard distress or has tried to roll, prevent his going down by walking him for a few minutes. You might need to use a whip to keep him on his feet. If he's not out of control, you can place him in cross-ties, which will serve to keep his head up. Massage his head and neck, and talk to him in a quiet, calm voice. He needs your reassurance.

Under no circumstances should you allow a colicking horse access to food of any kind, but make sure he has access to water. *Do not try to treat a colicking horse yourself.* Some commonly used colic medicines are 100 percent fatal if inappropriately administered. Mineral oil is easily inhaled, which may result in pneumonia and death. Some medicines simply mask the symptoms of colic, allowing the problem to worsen, undetected, for several life-threatening hours. Enemas are usually worse than useless for an adult horse, only causing further pain. A newborn foal may colic because of its inability to pass the meconium, or first fecal matter. It is recommended that foals that fail to pass this substance within six hours of birth receive an 8-ounce enema of mild soap and water.

If your horse suffers periodic bouts of colic, consult your veterinarian to determine the precise reason for the problem. Perhaps the horse's teeth need attention, or it is suffering parasite damage. Only a specific diagnosis allows effective treatment. Once a diagnosis is made, your vet may provide you with medication and instruct you regarding its proper dose and administration. If you're planning a pack trip deep in back country, where no veterinary help is available, you might ask your vet to provide you with some colic medicines, including pain killer and an antispasmodic colic remedy, to take along. These are absolutely the only times you should consider treating colic yourself.

Dental Problems

If your horse suddenly starts having trouble keeping weight on, dribbles grain or spits out half-chewed hay wads, if he turns his head in a curious sideways manner as he chews, or if his bit suddenly seems to cause pain, he may be having dental problems. As another warning sign, my vet warns that a horse's manure is a mirror image of his teeth. If an examination of the horse's manure reveals poorly digested hay or intact grain, you should suspect that his teeth aren't doing their job.

Horses three and four years old often need to have baby teeth or troublesome permanent teeth removed. Animals nine years or older are apt to develop sharp pointed hooks on their molars, which need to be filed down. This process is known as floating a horse's teeth. A veterinarian or equine dental technician can perform these procedures, as can a few specially trained farriers. Ask around your horse community to find out how to locate a reliable person to care for your horse's teeth.

Respiratory Distress

Horses are prone to a chronic respiratory illness commonly known as heaves. The horse with heaves may suffer a continual deep, dry cough; his nostrils will flare out when he breathes—even at rest. A more telling symptom is expiratory lift, when the horse, upon breathing out, pushes hard with his abdominal muscles in a futile attempt to empty his lungs, creating the characteristic "heaving" motion that gives this disease its name. An animal that has suffered enough from this disease will develop a thick ridge of muscles, known as a heave line, along the bottom edge of the rib cage, a result of the extra work these muscles do when the horse breathes.

Heaves is a chronic, progressive disease that is often caused by an allergic reaction to dust or mold, which is most often found in poor-quality hay. Clean, well-cured and well-stored hay is extremely important to the diligent horsekeeper. A horse will not develop sensitivities to substances he's never exposed to, and an existing lung condition will not worsen if further exposure is prevented.

Heaves can usually be managed but cannot be cured. If your horse is coughing or showing any kind of respiratory distress, allow the animal complete rest. Feed only good hay and, even then, dampen it with water before offering it to a horse that's prone to heaves. Never feed such a horse from overhead nets or racks, which increases the amount of dust the animal breathes in. Some horses cannot tolerate hay at all, but do well on a completely pelleted ration.

One of the best treatments for heaves is to allow the affected horse plenty of free access to clean pasture. Stall-bound horses are much more likely to develop heaves.

If these simple measures don't quickly eliminate the heaving, call your veterinarian. It might be necessary to treat an underlying viral infection. Some veterinarians, like mine, have developed techniques that help keep this troublesome disease under control.

General Malaise

If your horse is listless, having trouble breathing, has a clear or mucousy discharge from his mucous membranes, is coughing or has gone off his feed, you'll need to take note of these facts and then determine and record the horse's vital signs. All of this information will help your vet determine how serious the condition is and enable him to tell you how to proceed. Vital signs include the animal's pulse and respiration rates, temperature, capillary refill time and hydration.

PULSE. Find your horse's pulse by pressing the balls of your middle three fingers hard along the bottom, deeply curved inside edge of his jawbone. Investigation will reveal a rope-like artery that should yield a pulse. You also might be able to detect a pulse by pressing the back of

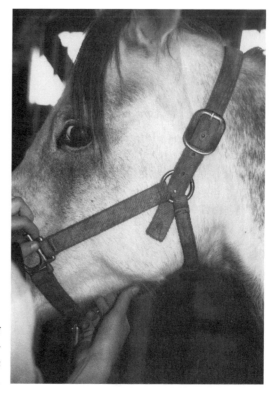

Fingertip exploration along the horse's jawline should reveal a rope-like artery, from which you can feel a pulse.

your hand hard against the horse's side, immediately behind the elbow, or by pressing your ear to this spot. It's ideal if you can acquire a stethoscope, which you should place behind the horse's elbow.

Once you've found the pulse—familiarize yourself with this procedure before illness strikes—count the number of beats for 20 seconds, and multiply that number by 3. An adult horse's normal resting pulse rate is usually between 26 and 40 beats per minute. It should not rise higher than 60 beats per minute. Expect a horse younger than three to have a considerably higher pulse—perhaps as high as 80 beats per minute. Make a note of what is normal for your horse when he's healthy, for comparison when he becomes injured or ill.

RESPIRATION.   Respiration rate is the number of complete breaths taken in one minute. One inhalation and one exhalation counts as a single complete breath. To count respiration, stand back and count the number of times the horse breathes in (or out), as indicated by the rising and falling of his rib cage. Normal resting respiration for a horse runs between 8 and 16 breaths per minute, perhaps higher in young or excited animals or during hot weather. Note what's normal for your horse.

TAKING A TEMPERATURE.   Every horseman ought to keep a large animal rectal thermometer equipped with a ring on one end. To the ring, attach a length of heavy nylon thread. Tie an alligator clip to the other end of the thread. To use: Vigorously snap and shake the thermometer down and spread petroleum jelly liberally on the end with the metal tip. Stand very close to the horse's left hip, facing rearward. Lift his tail with your left hand and carefully insert the thermometer into the rectum with your right, until only about one-half inch of the thermometer is exposed. Use the alligator clip to attach the thermometer to the hairs at the root of the horse's tail, so that the instrument won't accidentally get sucked up into the animal's rectum or knocked to the floor and broken should the horse swish his tail. Leave the thermometer in for two or three minutes, then unclip it from the tail, grasp the string and carefully remove it from the rectum.

Wipe the instrument off with a handful of straw, hay or tail hair before reading it. Normal temperature for the horse is between 99.5 and 101.4 degrees Fahrenheit, again possibly slightly higher for younger animals, during very hot weather or if the animal is excited. Keep a record of what is normal for your horse.

CAPILLARY REFILL.   Capillary refill time indicates how efficiently your horse's circulatory system is working. To determine capillary refill time, lift your horse's upper lip and press your thumb, hard, into his upper gum. When you lift your thumb, it will leave a whitish impression. Count the seconds it takes for the gum to return to its normal, pink color. One second is fine; three or four may indicate a problem.

While you're looking at the gums, note their color. They should be a healthy pink. Dark-red, bluish, black or white gums suggest trouble and should be reported to your veterinarian along with other vital signs.

HYDRATION.   To determine if your horse is dehydrated, lift a pinch of skin on the horse's neck. When suddenly released, the skin should be elastic enough to pop right back into place. If the skin stands up and takes more than one second to regain its original contour, the horse is

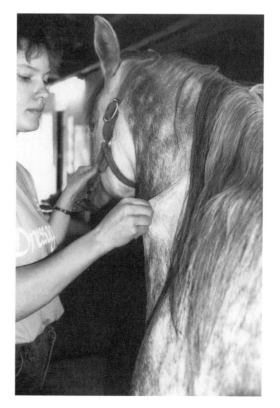

To determine hydration, lift a pinch of skin on the neck, then release. The skin should immediately return to its normal contours. If it stands up for one second or longer, the horse is dehydrated.

dehydrated. Be especially sure your horse has access to water if he's dehydrated.

PREVENTIVE HEALTH PRACTICES

Measures can be taken to prevent injury to your horse. Use the sturdiest, safest fencing material you can afford. Purchase and use tack that fits, keep it clean and condition your horse to its use gradually. Check fences often, and repair breaks or weak spots immediately. Accustom horses to traffic by tying them regularly near passing traffic or by arranging pasture feeders near a roadway (this helps ensure the rider's safety as well as the horse's).

Keep barn and pasture areas free of hazardous materials such as old batteries, kids' sleds, auto parts, rusty buckets, empty paint, kerosene or

Learn safe ways to handle and tie your horse. This horse is tied short enough to prevent tangling, the haynet is high so the animal can't get his foot bound in it, and the horse is wearing protective shipping wraps on all four legs.

antifreeze containers. Horses are curious and prone to sudden skittish moves, so leaving debris around in horse pastures is tantamount to inviting injury.

Remember to keep horse grains stored securely away from stall areas of the barn, and never allow a horse that is still hot from exercise to drink his fill of water. Groom your horse regularly, and get to know what is normal behavior for him. Learn safe ways to handle and tie your horse. Always maintain a calm attitude, but be ready for any kind of emergency.

Every horse owner should have several items on hand in his equine medicine chest. Here is a list of some of those items. No doubt you'll also want others.

bandages, gauze, duct tape, elastic Ace bandages
clean cotton rags
scissors

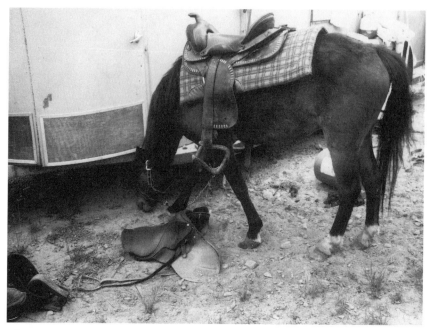

This scene is an accident waiting to happen. The horse is tied too long by a rope with a long chain shank. The chain could cause severe damage should the horse get tangled up in it and panic. Saddles and other paraphernalia should not be carelessly left within reach of the horse's feet. If he accidentally steps on something, it may cause him to spook and fight his restraints.

hoof knife (very sharp)
hoof dressing
insect spray
petroleum jelly
antiseptic soap
antiseptic spray or lotion (containing Nitrofurazone)
antifungal spray or powder (for fungal skin infections)
tincture of iodine (7% solution)
Epsom salts
copper sulphate solution (for treating thrush)
large animal thermometer (equipped as described above)
stethoscope

Ten

DISCIPLINE

AND TRAINING

A farrier was servicing a fractious horse. The woman who owned the animal stood at its head, apologizing for her horse's misbehavior.

"Why do you suppose some horses act up like this?" she asked the farrier.

"Well, I don't know for sure, but I have a theory. I think it might be something to do with their names."

"Their names?" asked the woman. "How could a horse's name have any effect on its behavior?"

"Well, like I said, I'm not really sure," said the farrier, standing up and wiping his brow with the sleeve of his shirt. He was sweating profusely from the effort of working under the horse, who kept leaning his entire weight on the poor man's back. "But it's a real curiosity to me how all the troublesome horses on my route seem to share the same name."

"How can that be? What name is that?" asked the woman. Just then, her horse reared back. She gave a worried little tug on the lead line, and said, "Please, honey, don't."

"That's it!" cried the farrier.

"That's what?" asked the woman, perplexed.

"That's the name I've been talkin' about. It's the most amazing thing—most of the troublesome horses I know are named Honeydont!"

THE NEED FOR DISCIPLINE

This story may be amusing, but there is nothing funny about an undisciplined horse. A horse that is allowed to bully, bluff and intimidate

123

people will become unpleasant and dangerous. On the other hand, one that is consistently and firmly disciplined will be a safe, pleasant animal to work around.

Horses are big, strong animals. To subdue them to our will, we must use some sort of restraint, one that goes beyond a weak ineffectual plea such as "honey, don't." The best restraint we can use is a device located under and between the equine's two ears: his brain. We discipline the horse's mind.

Contrary to popular misconception, the word discipline is not synonymous with the word punishment. Discipline is, simply put, obtaining subjection to authority by means of training, control and exercise. We train a horse to our control and then exercise, or practice, that control until the animal has developed an ingrained habit of obedience.

LEARNING TO COMMUNICATE

The first thing to establish with any horse is our authority. Obviously, we can't do this by outmuscling the animal. We've got to use our heads and learn to talk to the horse in a language he understands. Since the horse's natural responses are based primarily upon instinct, we must use his own instinctive responses to our advantage. In effect, we learn horse talk.

Horses use body language to establish and maintain herd hierarchy. Can you tell from the photo which horse is dominant and which submissive?

Horses use body language to communicate among themselves and to establish herd hierarchy. A dominant horse moves with bold confidence. To establish or maintain authority he occasionally uses aggression, displayed by means of confrontation; the dominant animal forces another to move out of his way, or bend to his will, using the threat of physical pain. Less dominant horses exhibit subjection by running away, turning aside or otherwise avoiding the aggressor. A boss horse refuses to back off from any perceived threat to his (or, quite often, her) authority and thus maintains authority over other members of the herd. Eventually herd members no longer seriously challenge that rule but accept it, and peace reigns in the pasture.

As handlers, we need to establish ourselves as boss horse, or the ultimate authority figure, in our horses' lives. Once that authority is established, we will be able to enjoy peaceable human/equine relationships, but not until that time. To establish our rule, we must at all times display confidence and even on occasion resort to aggression.

This doesn't mean that we bully our horses into submission. Our aggression should be of the benign variety and never result in serious injury or emotional trauma to the animal. The object is to generate respect, and an animal, including the human animal, will not respect someone it fears. Both horse and human reserve true respect for the person who demonstrates ability, understanding and patience.

The successful horse handler maintains a balance between the extremes of bullying and timidity. He demonstrates that he is able to make the animal do what he asks. At the same time, he is patient with the horse, resists asking for too much too fast, and never loses his temper or resorts to harsh treatment. He uses just as much force as is necessary—and not one iota more. He is quick but not lavish with rewards for good behavior and immediately sets up effective roadblocks for bad behavior.

Roadblocks and rewards. These are the secrets to effective horse discipline and training. We make it easy and rewarding for the horse to do what we want him to do, and difficult and punishing for him to do anything else.

ESTABLISHING AUTHORITY

What follows is a basic sequence for establishing authority, in other words, training a horse to obedience. This sequence and these methods are useful whether you are working with a fully grown and well-trained horse, a young horse or one that's been mishandled and spoiled. If the horse is already a trained, mature animal, you will be able to make rapid progress as you walk through these steps to establish your authority. Though already trained, the horse will still be learning. You may choose to skip over some steps, but I encourage you to run through most of what is described below. Whatever you're working on, observe the animal and proceed according to the horse's reactions, understanding and ability.

If the animal you're working with is young, plan to move along slowly, and be willing to back up a step if it seems you've asked for too much. It's usually best to resist the temptation to take on the training of a young animal until you've had a couple years' experience with horses, although an older, spoiled horse is often a greater danger to the novice than most youngsters. If you're working with an animal that's been spoiled, you'll need to muster all the self-confidence and determination possible. If you feel seriously intimidated or in danger from such a horse, send him out to a professional trainer.

A badly spoiled horse is no job for a novice, although you may work through minor problems on your own and almost surely will need to, from time to time. Even if the horse is too badly spoiled for you to handle on your own, be sure to take an active role in any retraining effort. It does little good if the animal learns to respect and obey the professional trainer but doesn't transfer these responses to his owner.

STANDING TIED

Assuming that any horse you purchase has had at least basic halter training, the first thing you'll need to teach your horse is to stand tied. Tying lessons may sound easy, but that's only if you forget one basic premise: The horse's main defense is swiftly running away from danger. Therefore, horses often instinctively fight any restraint as if it were a matter of life and death. It's our job to teach them that being tied is nothing to get excited about. It is safe—and unavoidable.

Use a sturdy nylon halter whenever your horse is to be tied. Leather will break or snap more easily than rugged nylon. Tie to a well-set stout post or to a tree, as horses exert a tremendous amount of power when they fight restraints. They must not be successful in pulling loose; if they

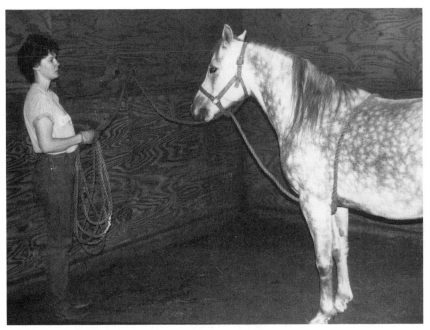

This horse is tied with a heavy belly rope, which is run through the halter to a secure anchor in the wall. A tree or well-anchored post will serve the same purpose. The handler stays nearby in case of trouble.

are, a life-long habit of halter pulling will result. Besides, if a horse pulls a fence board or post from the ground and tears off dragging it behind him, the board or post can cause a great deal of damage to the horse, as well as a tremendous amount of fear. The tie post should be free of any nails or other sharp objects that might injure the horse, and be high enough so the animal won't impale himself on it if he panics and jumps up and forward. The area around the post or tree must also be free of dangerous debris.

If your horse already ties, then simply tie him to a good, stout post on a regular basis, just to keep him in the habit of tying. If the horse doesn't tie or tries to pull back when tied, try the following: Use a 20' length of 2"-thick nylon plaited rope. Tie a fixed loop in one end of the rope, using a sturdy square knot. Loop the rope over the horse's back just behind the withers and then under the belly, just behind the elbow. Slip the free end of the rope through the loop at the other end and pull until the loop is snug around your horse's girth. You have in effect placed a noose around your horse's belly.

Now run the free end of the rope up between your horse's front legs to the halter. Thread this through the bottom ring of the halter, and use a quick-release knot to tie to the post or tree. Leave 12″ to 14″ of rope between the tie and your horse's head, and tie it at withers height. This much rope allows your horse to move his head from side to side but prevents him from gaining the needed momentum for breaking free if he pulls back. Work around your tied horse as though nothing were out of the ordinary. Groom him and talk to him, do barn chores, whatever is usual. Under no circumstances should you ever scoot under the neck of a tied horse! If he suddenly rears up, you could be struck by his front feet and killed. If the horse fights the restraint, stand well back and watch. The noose around his barrel will tighten as he pulls back, and let loose only when he stops fighting and steps forward. He'll soon find that it's more comfortable to stand quietly tied than it is to pull back. At that point, he'll quit fighting. In the meantime, always stay near a horse that is unaccustomed to being tied, and keep scissors or a sharp knife on hand, just in case he somehow gets tangled up and needs to be quickly rescued.

INSTILLING PATIENCE

Once your horse is used to being tied, teach him patience. Most young horses, when kept away from their herd mates, become very excited. They paw, holler out to one another and jump around. Some horses never get over this behavior but are a general nuisance everywhere they go, unless accompanied by their best friend. You don't want your horse to be like this.

This lesson is fairly easy to teach, so long as you're consistent and not overly intimidated by an excited horse. Simply keep your horse tied and separated from his herd mates on a regular basis. At first, you can turn all other horses except yours out to pasture, while leaving yours tied securely in his stall. He'll jump and prance and posture, but pay him no attention. Give him some hay, then duck out of sight for a while, but not out of hearing range. Unless it's obvious he's tearing up the barn, stay away until he becomes considerably less frantic. Then go in, give him a brushing and turn him out. Repeat this procedure for a few days, until he no longer carries on when the other horses leave the barn.

Once this much has been accomplished, tie him in various places around the farm; tying to a horse trailer is a good choice, as he'll probably have to become accustomed to this sooner or later anyway. Other good places to tie are to a post or tree near a busy road or in a pasture where a tractor is running. Make certain, of course, that there is absolutely no way for the horse to escape, and always keep an eye on him until he's settled down.

By the time you're finished with these lessons, you will be able to tie the horse anywhere, at any time, with all sorts of activities and other horses around, without his becoming excited or upset.

STANDING STILL

You will also want to teach your horse to stand absolutely still, without restraint, as you groom him. Until you've established mind control, you still must use some sort of physical control, so place a halter and lead rope on the animal. In this case, however, do not tie the lead to a stationary object. If you tie the horse, then as soon as the restraint is removed, he is no longer under your control (in fact, he never was, being subject only to physical restraint). So, as you work your way around the horse with curry comb and brush, you let the loose lead dangle on the ground.

If your horse so much as moves one foot, immediately—all road-blocks must be immediate—stop grooming and push or pull against him to make moving in that direction difficult. Push using your body, pull using the lead line. When a horse pushes back against you, he is being aggressive. You should not back off, or he will have won the battle for authority. If your horse tends to respond with this sort of aggression, you must be prepared to counter it. Carry a crop or a short stout stick, and give him a calculated jab as he steps in toward you. He will instinctively move away from the threat of pain, and it will seem to him that his disobedient movement, rather than your presence, resulted in punishment.

Once the horse has been placed back in the exact spot he was in before moving, give him a business-like pat, and go on grooming. No matter how often the horse attempts to move, patiently repeat this procedure. Some mischievous horses may try to make a game of this. If yours does, don't waste a minute on anger or recriminations, as the horse, like a child who's being yelled at by a noisy, fearful parent, will quickly see through your bluff. Simply repeat this simple discipline as often as necessary, adding a sharp poke and quick reprimand if the horse continues challenging you. He will eventually realize it's less trouble to obey than it is to disobey.

STANDING AT A DISTANCE

The next step is to teach your horse to stand even when you move away from him. Start this lesson in an enclosed place, so the horse can't simply kick up his heels and run away. Place a halter and very long lead, or lunge line, on the horse. Wear gloves to protect your hands against rope burn, should the horse suddenly try to pull away, pulling the line through your hand. Never loop the lunge line around your hand, which could be caught up and injured if the line is suddenly pulled or jerked. Instead hold the line in coils, with your hand in the center, butterfly fashion. Now you can feed out as much line as you wish, while your hand remains free of entanglement.

Standing on the horse's left, carry a lungeing whip in your right hand and the lunge line in your left. Ask your horse to "stand," just as you do when grooming. Now deliberately back away from your horse, while still holding the lead. Repeat the command "stand" every time your horse moves.

If the horse tries to turn or step toward you, say "whoa!" and shake the end of the lead line. The unpleasant sensation of the shaking rope will serve as a roadblock. If he persists in moving, simply replace him where you want, as often as necessary. If he insists on moving in toward you after several attempts, slap him across the shoulder (*not* the rump!) with your lungeing whip. Once he's been disciplined, again settle him in place and ask him to stand.

A word of warning: As you move out away from the horse, there will be a critical period of time when you will be within the dangerous kill zone, or kicking range. Keep your whip at the ready and be on guard. Should the horse pin his ears back, hunch up and pull his legs underneath or raise a threatening leg on your side, immediately hit the threatening leg or legs—hard!—with your whip. He must know that you absolutely will not tolerate kicking. Most animals won't kick, except

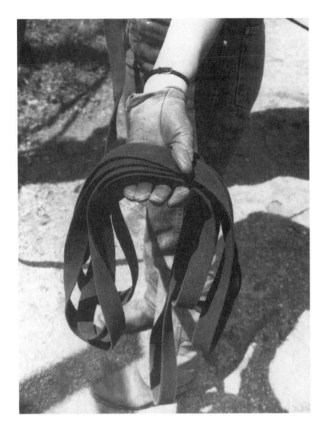

Always wear gloves and handle the lunge line "butterfly" fashion when working a horse. Looping lines around your hand can cause you to be seriously injured if the horse fights, or panics, and pulls out hard on the line.

defensively. If yours continues to threaten in this way, you may have gained ownership of a rogue.

When your horse stands still for you at a four-foot distance, move back in and pet and praise him, then increase the distance to six feet. Soon he'll be standing obediently on command at any distance. Then repeat the training, standing on the horse's right side (this helps prevent a one-sided horse). The training sequence is always the same: Ask for a certain response; if necessary, reinforce your request with aggression and the use of his instinctual response to move away from threatened pain; and immediately reward desired behavior.

LESSONS IN LEADING

Intersperse the lesson in standing with leading lessons. Most horses will lead, but you want your horse to lead *correctly*. This means you don't actually *lead* the horse by pulling from the front at his head but rather move alongside the animal, about a foot and a half from his shoulder. The horse moves in a straight line at the same speed that you move, and will "walk," "trot" or "whoa" immediately upon command. He neither crowds into you nor pulls away from you but synchronizes his movements to yours.

To accomplish all this, you'll need a straight barrier, such as a wall or fence, at least 30 feet long. Position yourself at the horse's shoulder at one end of this wall or fence, with his other side parallel to the barrier. Carry the lead line in your gloved hand, the hand closest to the horse. Hold this about one foot from where it snaps onto the halter's side ring,

Teach your horse to lead along a fence line or other straight barrier, using a lungeing whip behind (as shown) to tap the horse forward when necessary. Ask for "whoa" when the horse reaches the corner.

so that the horse's head is free to move up and down naturally. Carry a lungeing whip in your other hand, keeping the butt end in your hand and the whip end facing down and slightly behind you.

Give the command "walk," and start to move, slowly. If your horse doesn't move with you, don't get ahead of him and start tugging at his head. Instead remain at the horse's shoulder and move the lungeing whip farther *behind* you. Tap it lightly just below the horse's hocks. Be prepared for the horse to lunge forward. If he does, simply restrain his forward motion with the lead rope until you are both walking. If the horse tries to rush forward, restrain him with the lead; if he tries to lag behind or stop, tap him with the lungeing whip. If he crowds you, give a shake of the lead rope; if that's not enough to push him off, then give his shoulder a sharp poke with the butt end of the lungeing whip.

At first all of this will feel awkward, but don't worry—you'll get coordinated long before the horse does. Before long he will discover it's most rewarding to walk along beside you, keeping a reasonable distance. Now teach him to lead from the other side.

Teach the horse to stop on command by saying "whoa" as you reach the far end of the barrier, resisting his forward motion with your hand on the lead rope. The first few times you may actually have to tug hard to get him to stop, unless, of course, you are walking him along a barrier *into* a barrier, such as a fence corner. Then he'll have no recourse except to stop on command, as his body will be trapped between you and the corner of the fence.

Once he's moving along obediently at the walk and stopping on command, introduce the command "trot." After he's started walking, say "trot!" in a sharp, commanding tone, and start to move faster yourself. If he doesn't immediately pick up the gait himself, again use your lungeing whip behind you to tap below his hocks until he changes gait. Be patient, but also be willing to tap a sluggish horse a bit harder than you would when you were merely asking him for a walk. A more spirited animal will need hardly any extra encouragement; you may, in fact, need extra restraint to prevent such a horse from getting excited and breaking away. In such a case, use the lead shank chain at the end of your lead rope up over the horse's nose, twisted once around the halter noseband and clipped to the off side upper halter ring. If the horse tries to pull ahead of you, a few sharp tugs on the lead shank chain will keep him in line and help keep his mind on business. You should use a few sharp tugs rather than a continuous hard pull because it is never a good idea to get into a pulling contest with your horse. He'll win every time.

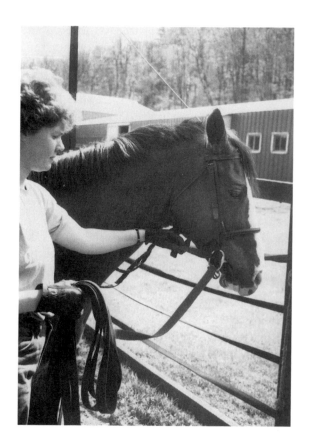

A snaffle bridle may be used for lungeing a horse.

LUNGEING LESSONS

Now that your horse is standing still at a distance and is well acquainted with "walk," "trot" and "whoa" commands, it's time to begin lungeing lessons.

When teaching a horse to lunge, our connection for physical control is the head harness. This should be a lungeing cavesson or snaffle bridle. A lungeing cavesson is the best choice. A snaffle bridle is good for a horse who already has some training to the bridle, but only if you have very sensitive hands, as lungeing with a bit in place can toughen a horse's mouth. Many people use a simple halter for lungeing, but this is a poor choice. The halter usually slips around on the horse's head and can easily injure an eye. Besides this, a halter offers the handler very little control, a fact that most horses soon learn to take advantage of. A sturdy nylon cavesson may be purchased for less than $20 and is well worth the price.

Carry a long (30-foot) lunge line and the lungeing whip. Work in an area where the horse's physical escape routes are limited, such as a 50- or 60-foot-wide round pen or the corner of a corral or arena. If you have no such facility, create one using temporary posts and clothesline. Any barrier, even if it is only a metal barrier for the horse, is better than none.

To lunge the horse to the right, stand on the horse's right side holding the (butterflied) lunge line in your (gloved) right hand, the whip in your left. Demonstrate what you expect of the horse by leading him

Proper lungeing position of horse and handler, as viewed from above. The handler remains opposite the horse's hip while the horse is moving forward. The horse's body is contained between the line and the lungeing whip.

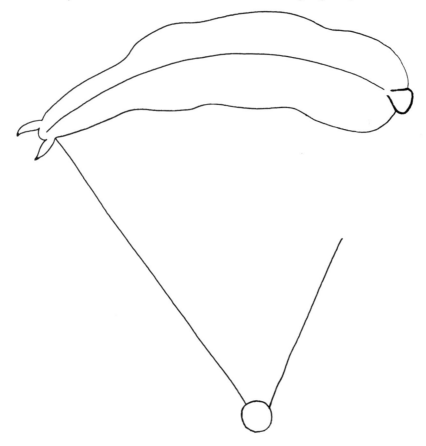

around a circle two or three times. Then stop, and ask him to stand while you move backward toward the center of the circle. This routine should be familiar to him.

Once you reach the center of the circle, at least ten feet distant, stand parallel to the horse's hip. Position the lunge line and lungeing whip so the horse's body is between the two. Now, say "walk," and tap the horse below the hock with the lungeing whip. At the same time move your upper right side subtly in toward his hip, as though chasing him (again, beware of the kill zone). If the horse attempts to turn in and face toward you—as he almost surely will, at least once or twice—shake the lead rope as discouragement and persist in asking him for forward movement by tapping below the hocks and using swooping chase motions toward his hip. If this fails to stop him from turning in, sweep the tip of the lungeing whip across his barrel to his shoulder, which will serve to literally push him out away from you.

About the use of the whip: Never use it to actually whip or punish the horse. Such tactics produce fear, and a fearful frame of mind is not conducive to learning. Nevertheless, the horse must consider any such device a barrier, or roadblock, to undesired behavior. An animal who has learned whips are capable of producing an unpleasant sting will not challenge them but will tend to move away from them to avoid an unpleasant sensation. This is the conditioned response you want. So long as the horse is obedient, you need not inflict any unpleasantness. If he acts as though he's going to refuse your command, shake or snap the whip as warning, much as another horse might bare his teeth or lift a hind leg as warning. If this doesn't produce the desired response, then use the whip as a physical barrier, one that causes some amount of pain. In the equine world, a boss horse would bite or kick a recalcitrant herd mate. Such physical discipline, however, must come immediately upon the horse's disobedience, so that he associates the pain with his disobedience, rather than with the trainer.

Some horses require greater reinforcement to learn this lesson. On the other hand, a sharp rap that barely fazes a stubborn animal might send a sensitive creature into a fearful frenzy. Use your powers of observation to ascertain how much persuasion your horse requires to learn respect for the lungeing whip. Always start with the least amount of discipline and escalate from that point.

If you are a short-fused, hot-headed person who cannot control the impulse to punish an animal for misbehavior, you should lay down your whip and turn all training over to a professional. Horses are slow to forget a beating and only too quick to seize any opportunity for revenge. One inappropriate discipline may set the horse's training back several weeks or months, irrevocably damage your relationship with the animal and cause him to mistrust all humans forever.

When your horse first starts moving on the circle to lunge, his gaits and pace will be somewhat erratic. He'll be rushing around, stopping, veering in and out. This is all right. Don't expect immediate understanding and control. When he becomes more accustomed to this routine, he'll settle down.

As the horse lunges, follow his movements around the circle, keeping your body parallel to his hip, with his body between your line and whip. Actually, you too are walking a circle, only a much smaller one than the horse. Remember, we want to use body language to speak to the horse. Staying at his hip in effect pushes him around the circle. When you request "whoa," you change position so that you have stepped forward of the horse's head, while still maintaining a position inside the circle.

When first teaching the horse to stop on the lunge line, move so that your request to "whoa" coincides with his coming up against a barrier, such as a fence. Soon, the word "whoa" and the barrier set up by your body language as you move toward the front of his body will be all the command he needs. If he forgets or challenges you when you ask him to stop without the additional reinforcement of a physical barrier, simply step toward his head and threaten him by snapping the lungeing whip across the space in front of his chest. This movement will stop most horses. If he needs more reinforcement, pop the whip against his chest.

Should the horse whirl around and start running in the opposite direction, stop him, calmly turn him around and start over. The idea is for the horse to obey your commands, and he must change course only on your say-so. Remember to stay calm, even if the horse doesn't. The more panicky the horse, the more he needs his handler's reassurance that everything is OK.

Once the horse is walking and stopping on command, let him pick his pace up to a trot. Most horses will want to break into a trot from time to time, anyway. Once the horse is under control on the line, you should be able to prevent this by saying "easy," and stepping toward the horse's head, thereby slowing down progress. Don't ever command "whoa!" unless you want that horse to *plant it!* One of the most im-

Use your body language to drive the horse forward on the lungeing circle . . .

. . . and to stop the horse when lungeing.

portant lessons your horse must learn is that "whoa!" *always* means "stop right now!"

When you're ready to teach him to trot on the line, on command (as he already does when being led), you can take advantage of his inclination to break into a faster gait. Watch the horse to anticipate when he's going to break, then give a snap of the whip, scoot your body toward his hip and say "trot!" He'll do what he planned to do anyway, only you've made him think it was at your command.

Once you begin work, don't allow too many lapses in training. You must work with the horse to reinforce what he's learned and to add onto this foundation of knowledge at least every other day. If you can't give the work this much time, pay a professional trainer who will. A horse in training that's not being used is an animal that's being spoiled for use.

If you work every day, within about a week the horse should be lungeing in both directions and obeying the "walk," "trot" and "whoa" commands. But remember, every horse is an individual, and learning tempos and styles differ greatly. Be sensitive to your horse's messages. If his body language and eyes tell you one day that he's weary, then give him a one-day break. When you go back to training, be extra careful to keep the lessons short, and varied. A smart, bored horse will just look for mischief. If it takes three weeks for the horse to learn to listen and obey the simplest command, that's OK, too. Often the slowest-learning animals turn out to be extremely trustworthy mounts, if we don't get impatient and make them fearful.

You shouldn't try to move the animal on to more strenuous work, such as cantering, until he's had several weeks of regular lunge work to condition his bones, tendons and muscles. Also, at no time should you overdo lunge work, as working in a circle places a lot of stress on the animal's lower legs. Start with five minutes to each side, and always work the horse both ways, although most animals are resistant to working in one direction or the other. Be very persistent about this. Over two or three weeks, graduate to about fifteen minutes of work in each direction, unless the horse is less than two years old. In that case, limit lunge work to twenty minutes, total. Lunge work should not begin until the animal is at least a yearling, and should start out with five- to ten-minute lessons, not only because of the physical stress of the work, but also because young horses have short attention spans. Lessons must be kept fresh, interesting and varied. Also, make sure the horse gets a good grooming following a workout, and check him over carefully for any evidence of soreness or stress injuries.

SACKING OUT AND SADDLING

Now is the ideal time to sack out the horse in preparation for introducing the saddle. After your horse has had his lunge work, tie him up stout and place a saddle pad on his back. Rub it around on top of him, then move it down to his belly and rub some more. Move it all over his body. Once he's accepted this, slap it around on his back and rump, keeping yourself out of the way of trouble, of course. This routine, known as sacking out, teaches a horse that it's all right to be touched all over with equipment. If the horse accepts sacking out pretty well, you can move right on to the saddle. If not, give him another day or two.

When he seems ready for more, place the left stirrup up over the saddle horn of an old saddle. The horse must still be tied during these lessons; otherwise he may roll in an attempt to rid himself of the saddle, which could damage his withers and back, to say nothing of the saddle. Introduce the saddle from the off, or right side of the horse, as this eliminates the need to tangle with the latigo and cinch strap. Very gently place the saddle on the horse's back, over the saddle pad. Talk to the horse reassuringly. Make the experience as pleasant as possible.

Once it seems pretty certain he won't blow up, grab the saddle horn and cantle, and pull the saddle around on his back, as you did with the saddle blanket—back and forth, up and down, reassuring him all the while. When he's sufficiently relaxed, carefully move around to his left side, reach underneath his belly and grab the cinch. Cautiously bring it up to be tied. Do not cinch up too tightly; pull the cinch only as snug as necessary to hold the saddle in place, and do even this in stages. Under no circumstances must the horse feel a sudden sharp pressure around his barrel, or he will certainly panic and fight.

Once the saddle is on, stick around and do a few barn chores. Let him discover for himself that the saddle won't suddenly attack with tooth and claw. Give the horse his ration of grain, which helps him associate this new experience with something pleasant. When the horse seems ready, the next step is to lunge him with the saddle on. Start him out at a walk, and work him this way in both directions. Then tighten the cinch a bit more, in preparation for work at the trot. Be prepared for a few surprised bucks or maybe even outright rebellion the first few times the saddle and stirrup fenders bounce around, but stick to your agenda and insist that he move out on the circle. Before long, he'll pay the saddle no attention whatever.

Start to intersperse his lungeing lessons with other kinds of play. Here are some exercises that will help prepare the horse for many different experiences.

LEADING FROM A 10-FOOT DISTANCE. This is simple enough, actually, and a lot of fun. As you're lungeing one day, simply start walking a straight line, rather than in a circle. Use your lunge line and whip, preferably along a barrier, to encourage the horse to move along with you. Most horses really enjoy this, and it prepares them for the next lesson.

LINE DRIVING. Attach a loop of twine or rubber to the latigo on either side of your saddle. This will be used to run your long lines through, or you may use a surcingle for this lesson, rather than a saddle. Attach a lunge line to the left cavesson ring or through the left ring of a simple snaffle bridle.

With the left line in hand, walk around the horse and attach a lunge line of a different color to the right side of the horse's head device. Run this line through the side ring of the saddle or surcingle. Lay the excess right-hand line up on the saddle horn or surcingle.

Standing close on the horse's left side, with the left line in your hand, carefully take the right side line and loop it over your horse's back and down the other side. Still standing on the left, bring the right-hand line back to the horse's haunches and behind his buttocks. The first time this is attempted, the feel of the line over his buttocks may spook the horse; be sure to keep the left-hand line in your hand, so you can simply move him out and control him at the end of the lunge line until he settles down, if necessary.

Introduce the line at his rear with reassuring pats to the hip and buttock region. Once he's standing still for the line, rub it around on his buttocks to get him accustomed to that feel.

With a line in each hand and a lungeing whip in your right hand, move back from the horse while feeding both lines and ask him to lunge. Besides the lunge line and whip for control, you now have a line that is attached through a side ring to the other side of his cavesson or bridle that runs around his buttocks to your hand. As the horse lunges on the circle, let this second line hang fairly loose at first, but not so loose that it hangs down and rubs against his legs.

If the horse panics at this juncture and starts to fight, let go of the

141

To attach a second long line for line driving a horse, maintain control with a direct line from one side. Carefully slip the second line around the horse's opposite side and buttocks. This horse is sporting a training cavesson and body surcingle. Both devices are helpful for attaching training lines and devices.

right-hand line and take control with the left. This is the reason we don't run the left line through the latigo or surcingle ring. We can still take direct control of the horse. Working with a single line from the head harness will be a familiar routine, and you should be able to calm the horse down and prevent the two of you from becoming hopelessly snarled in two lines. If a tangle should develop, the differently colored lines will help you easily distinguish which side is which. Once the horse has settled down after a blowup, stop him. Repeat the two-line procedure until he is moving on the circle to the left easily with both lines. If he tries to turn in toward you, give a tug on the outside line to pull his head away. Repeat this training to the right, leaving the line on the right side free from the loop off the latigo or surcingle ring.

Once the horse lunges easily with both lines, start leading him with them from a distance, as described above. Gradually move farther and farther back and behind the horse, until he's traveling well out in front

Start work on double lines by lungeing as usual, using the direct inside line for control. Gradually accustom the horse to the outside line's action by using it to prevent him from tipping his nose into the circle. As he gets used to two lines, move from the lungeing position to one at least 8 feet behind the horse. Ground driving teaches a horse to balance, stop, turn and back in response to rein aids. It is also useful for exposing the horse to new stimuli.

of you (and you're out of kicking range). Use your lungeing whip to keep forward motion, and the long lines to turn his head in either direction.

Congratulations! You've now got your horse under saddle, under your control, and ready for almost anything! Take a month—or six!—to accustom the horse to all sorts of new experiences before being mounted. With the long lines and a saddle, walk him through high grass, over bridges, around traffic and through water and mud. Teach him to walk, stop, turn and back at your command. Attach a couple of big feed bags filled with sawdust, or old tires, to the saddle horn, so the bags or tires straddle the saddle, one falling to either side. Now teach the horse to lunge and long line while carrying this additional floppy burden. An interactive human rider will seem like a piece of cake to your horse after he's had experience with these kinds of dummies.

THE BRIDLE

There's one more lesson the horse must learn before you step up into the saddle. It's time to introduce the bridle. (See pages 146–147.)

Though many professional trainers use a bosal to start a horse, I prefer to start a horse right out in a mild-jointed snaffle bit bridle. The horse will need to become accustomed to a bit at some point anyway. The first time I slip the snaffle into the horse's mouth, it's covered with molasses. He literally learns to eat it up from my hand. I'm very careful about slipping the headstall on. I don't want to hit an eye with the browband, or pin an ear under the crown piece. For a jumpy horse it's best to unfasten one cheek piece, slip the bit into the horse's mouth, pull the leathers into place and rebuckle the cheek piece. Whether or not this is necessary depends, of course, on the horse.

BRIDLING SEQUENCE

Once the bridle is in place, without reins, I let the horse wear it in his stall for a half to three-quarters of an hour; I repeat this for three or four days. Then I tie him in his stall, saddle and bridle him, attach rope or rubber reins to the rings of the snaffle, and then untie him. The reins are pulled loosely back and attached to the D-ring of the saddle on both sides. One side is left very loose, while the opposing side is tied so that the horse's head is pulled into a *very slight* bend. I can't emphasize "very slight" enough. Too much pressure and the horse will panic and fight. At the worst, he'll injure himself, especially his tender mouth; at best, he's learned to resist direct pressure on the bridle. We want to teach him to relax, and give his neck and head to the pull of the bridle.

The horse will usually circle around in the direction of the shortened side for a minute or two, until he discovers it's more comfortable to stand still and simply give his neck to the pressure of the rein. Once he's been quiet for about five minutes—again, I never overdo this lesson—I loosen the rein on the pressure side and tie the opposite rein ever so slightly shorter, so the lesson is repeated to both sides.

If the horse is left in this bitting rig for too long he'll learn, rather than giving to bridle pressure, to set his shoulder and neck muscles against that pressure. This is self-defeating. Being left in the rig for too long will make the horse confused and sore, and later on he'll become sulky, and strong. Such treatment strengthens both his will and his muscles for resistance to the bit. Never use a bitting rig for more than ten minutes, and never ask for more than a very slight bend in the horse's neck.

Line drive the horse for a few days using a snaffle bridle, with the snaps of the lunge line clipped to the rings of the snaffle. Keep in mind that your hands are now connected to his mouth, rather than just to side halter rings. After this exercise, there's little left to do except mount up. Given such slow, patient conditioning, most horses take their first mounting with equanimity.

MOUNTING UP

On a day when your horse is relaxed and willing, and maybe even a little bit tired, take the long lines off the bridle and attach a set of reins (clip-on reins are the most convenient). For safety's sake, attach a lead line to the halter, which should have been left on under the bridle. Place an assistant at the horse's head to hold the lead line. Your assistant might even offer the horse a tidbit as you go to the horse's side. Take the reins in hand. Slowly and very smoothly, step up into the stirrup. Step down. Repeat this procedure until he's obviously comfortable with it. Now after you've stepped up, lay across the saddle for a few seconds. Then step down again. Finally, mount up into the saddle, keeping as low a profile as possible, so that when you suddenly appear high above the horse's back he won't feel undue alarm. Sit quietly for a few minutes, then dismount. Pat his neck and tell him he was a good boy.

Next time, saddle up and again place the bridle over the halter. In an enclosed area, mount up carefully with the assistance of a friend. This time have your horse's halter attached to a lunge line, rather than a lead. After your assistant has moved to lungeing position, ask the horse to move off by saying "walk" and squeezing your calves against his barrel. If he doesn't move, repeat, and have your assistant reinforce your commands by lungeing him from the center of a circle. This system is the equivalent of the tightrope walker's safety net. It only makes sense that, as a nonprofessional trainer, you will do everything you can to make this experience a safe one. Within just a day or two you will be able to take over the controls, dispensing with the lunge lines and assistant altogether.

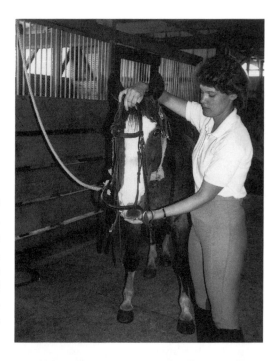

Place the halter over the horse's neck for control. Holding the bridle crown piece in your right hand, place your right arm over the horse's poll. The bridle will fall into the correct position down the length of the horse's face.

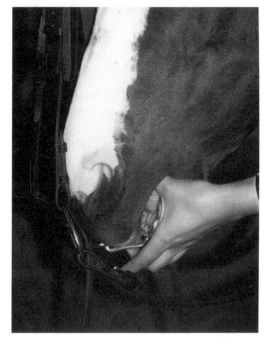

Holding the bridle in position with your right hand, slip the thumb of your left hand into the space at the bars (the toothless space) of the horse's mouth, and press down. This will cause the horse to open his mouth.

146

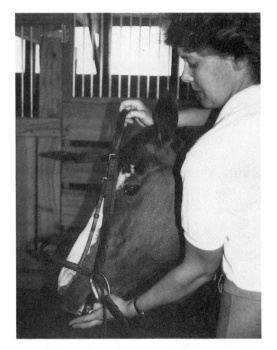

Once the horse opens his mouth, use your left hand to position the bit so it doesn't bang the horse's teeth; then pull up on the crown piece with your right hand. Carefully slip the crown piece over the horse's ears.

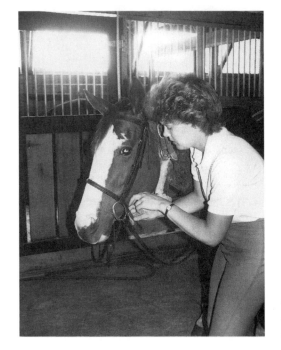

Check the bit and the bridle for correct fit and position. Secure all keepers (buckles and straps).

147

Once you're riding solo, practice walking your horse in circles and figure eights, using a leading rein or straight outward pull on the bridle, and very little leg pressure. Practice his transitions from stop to walk and then back to stop. Then begin working him at a trot. This will seem incredibly bouncy at first, but his trot will smooth out as he learns to balance himself while carrying a rider.

Start out with ten-minute riding sessions, increasing the time over two or three weeks until you're working the horse for a half hour. Over this period of time you'll be able to make your rein aids more subtle, until you're directing the horse using a direct rein and leg aids. As with all lessons, vary your routine and end your riding sessions on a positive note.

You'll be wise to arrange for an older, stable horse and rider to accompany you on your first few rides in the outside world. Ride with someone who can help keep things under control for your first road experience.

Nothing, but nothing, teaches a horse good sense and muscles him up like trail riding. Go out on the trail or through open, uncultivated fields as often as possible. If your riding must take you along roadsides, you should teach your horse beforehand to accept traffic by tying him to a sturdy tree near the road (but not closer than eight feet) for an hour or two every day. Better yet, arrange a pasture feeder so that it faces the road.

The last basic lessons you'll teach your horse are neck reining and backing up when mounted. Even if the horse is going to be ridden English-style, there are times when the ability to control him using only one hand will be essential. Besides, teaching a horse to neck rein is easy. For a right turn, use regular leg aids: Move your left foot slightly behind the girth to steady the horse's hindquarters and prevent them from swinging out. Your right leg presses into the horse's side at the girth. Now exert direct rein pressure by pulling slightly back on the right-hand rein. At the same time, bring the loose left-hand rein forward and across the horse's neck. In effect, the neck is being pushed in the direction of the turn. Reverse this process for a turn to the left. After you've done this a few times, give the neck rein first, and reinforce your neck reining cue with a direct rein only when necessary.

Practice this reining all the time, making deeper and deeper turns that demand greater and greater flexibility from the horse, until he associates the leg aids and rein pressure on the neck with turning. Gradually you can eliminate the direct rein altogether, if you so desire.

As for backing, many people have the mistaken notion that backing a horse means pulling on the reins until he backs up to relieve the pressure on his mouth. Unfortunately, too many horses have been trained this way. The truth is a horse that backs up properly does so only because he has good forward impulsion, or energy. Therefore it is important before attempting to teach a horse to back that he be consistently moving forward with an energetic stride. That's the reason for saving this training for last.

Once he has good forward motion, walk the horse to a fence or other barrier, and stop. Squeeze his barrel with both calves; as he steps into the bridle, refuse to give your hand to his forward motion, thus "catching" his energy. The fence, and the bridle, will resist his forward motion, so his energy will naturally take him backward. It's really that simple. In the beginning, if you can get him to so much as rock backward or take a single step back, pat his neck, praise him profusely and go on to other things. Gradually increase the amount of backing you require until it becomes as natural as anything else he's asked to do under saddle, and he'll do it anytime, anywhere.

It's best if a horse will back up in a straight line. Teach this by keeping one side of the horse against a barrier and using your outside leg to resist outward motion. But again, don't expect perfection until the horse is consistently moving back easily and willingly.

Nothing worthwhile is ever accomplished with a horse quickly. Good training—building a solid foundation and a trusting relationship—takes time, the amount varying with every animal. I trained one young gelding who learned everything the first time around so quickly that it seemed he must have been through it all before in some previous life. I also own an older trained mare that required eighteen months of regular work before she finally relaxed and settled down to trust me. To this day, she's a ball of fire under saddle, but a kind and obedient ball of fire.

Kindness, obedience and natural spiritedness—these qualities are the expected result of consistent, appropriate discipline and training.

Eleven

EQUESTRIAN

ETIQUETTE

*B*asic rules of etiquette govern the behavior of thoughtful equestrians. But unlike some arbitrary forms of social etiquette, such as deciding which fork to use at a formal dinner, most of the rules related to equestrian behavior have an important underlying purpose: to promote safe, enjoyable horsemanship. The lines between safety and etiquette often blur or become nonexistent. For that reason, this chapter deals with both issues.

If a horseman uses common sense in every situation involving horses and riders, he will almost certainly be doing the right thing. Let's see what this means in some typical situations.

GENERAL RULES OF BEHAVIOR

Whenever you are around horses, whether yours or someone else's, avoid sudden unexpected movements and/or loud noises that might startle a horse. When moving in close to a horse or passing around it, announce your presence and whereabouts. Avoid the kicking zone of an unfamiliar or unpredictable animal. Always be alert when around horses. Wear hard boots to protect your feet.

Don't presume an intimate relationship with someone else's animal, unless by express or clearly implied permission. Limit your petting to a simple pat or rub. Don't whisper sweet nothings in the ear of any horse other than your own or, worse yet, blow horse kisses into his nose. Not only might unwarranted familiarity incite jealous feelings on the part of the horse owner, but some animals answer overly friendly overtures with hostility.

Although most serious horse lovers are continually evaluating and comparing horse to horse and rider to rider, forming opinions about their relative merits, few of us appreciate the person who is quick to voice these opinions. Refrain from criticizing other horses and horse people unless you're a paid trainer or instructor. Ask questions, by all means, but avoid offering unsolicited criticism or advice. Most of us learn more by watching and listening than we do by talking.

Keep your horse's stall clean at all times, and your animal well groomed. This practice promotes good health and a sense of well-being for the horse, and goodwill from the stable owner, if you board your horse.

Your tack and grooming supplies should always be in good repair and kept separate from the belongings of other boarders. Borrowed curries, brushes, blankets or cinch straps can promote the spread of parasites. If you need to borrow tack, return it as soon as possible, making certain it is in as good condition as when you borrowed it, or better.

"Neither a borrower nor a lender be" is a lesson for the horseman too. If you are asked for the use of your horse, make it a habit to decline. You could be held responsible for anyone who is injured by your animal. Similarly, if you must lend tack, make certain it is in good repair, and lend it only if you are willing to lose it. Accidents happen and equipment is damaged or destroyed even under the best of circumstances. It is far easier to replace a saddle or bridle than it is a good friend.

Even more stringent rules apply to the use of a horse trailer. Frequently, owners of horse trailers are asked to transport horses, but our well-meaning friends and acquaintances don't know what they're asking. They seem to assume that hauling horses is no more complicated than moving a sofa or any other large object, but that is not the case. Many otherwise well-behaved horses are poor loaders, or travelers, and can do extensive damage to themselves and/or trailers. Trucks pulling loaded horse trailers sway with the movements of the animals, thus increasing the chances of an accident. Few auto insurance policies cover injuries to animals being hauled; if they do, they only cover injuries to animals belonging to the policy holder. For everyone's sake, if someone asks you to haul horses, refer them to a commercial horse transporter.

If you don't own a horse trailer, resist the temptation to ask for horse transportation as a favor from friends and acquaintances. Take my word for it, you'll be putting them on the spot. Hire a professional, or rent needed equipment. If you find yourself needing such transportation often, perhaps you should check into purchasing a horse trailer and/or appropriate hauling vehicle, and learn to transport your own animal.

BOARDING MANNERS

If you board your horse at a stable with limited riding facilities, use these facilities during off hours whenever possible. If you schedule lessons, try to schedule them for some time other than early Saturday afternoon. Scheduling weekday morning or early afternoon lessons not only helps a full-time instructor make good use of his time; it may result in your receiving more one-on-one, quality instruction than you could get during the busiest hours.

Keep up your end of any boarding arrangement. If you've agreed to pay a certain sum for board each month, pay it all, and on time. If part of your horse's board includes a work-for-services agreement, don't neglect to do the work, again on time.

If your boarding arrangement allows the stable owner to use your horse as part of the exchange agreement, make certain you know exactly what this means, agree to all points and, as with any boarding agreement, get it in writing. How many hours per month will your horse be used, and at how many dollars' benefit to yourself? How will he be used, and by whom? Will he be used strictly as a lesson horse, or can the owner's friend saddle your horse for a trail ride if she wants? Will your use of the horse be limited to times when he's not otherwise needed? In case of a conflict, who has first rights to use of the animal? You should insist that your horse not be handled and ridden by too many people, especially novice riders. You'll also want to make certain that, in case of a conflict, you always have first rights to the use of your own horse.

There are times when such agreements work fine, but on the whole I don't recommend them because there's too much room for misunderstandings to develop. It's also not generally good for a horse to be ridden regularly by a number of different people, with varying techniques, talents and levels of riding expertise. The horse may get hard-mouthed and will almost certainly become confused, which can lead to sluggishness or balking.

SAFETY CONSIDERATIONS

Riding boots should have good heels to prevent your feet from sliding through the stirrups and hanging you up in case of an accident. It makes good sense to wear a hard hat when riding. If your horse tends to kick at other horses, tie a red ribbon in his tail. This practice should be observed whether you are on the trail or in the riding arena. Furthermore, whether or not your horse is known to kick, always keep a safe distance from other animals. Maintain at least one and a half horse lengths, front and back, between your horse and another. If riders come up too close behind, give them a verbal warning. A defensive horse kick frequently lands on—and may shatter—the knee of the rider coming up behind, rather than on the offending horse. Though it may prejudice some riders or judges against your horse, don't hesitate to use the red ribbon. On trail rides with many people I sometimes tie one onto a horse that's perfectly harmless, just to prevent overly aggressive riders from coming up too close behind.

SHOWING RESPECT FOR PRIVATE PROPERTY

If riding cross country, make certain you have permission from landowners before setting so much as a foot on privately owned property. Even if the land isn't prominently posted, this policy will earn you high points and do horsemen everywhere a service. If a landowner refuses such permission, respect his or her right to do so, but try to leave the door open for future opportunity by remaining steadfastly courteous. You and your riding friends might even offer to help maintain trails on land you're allowed to use.

If a farmer gives you permission to ride on his land, make certain that you never cross fields that are cultivated. Also avoid upsetting livestock by passing as far away from them as possible. If you find a gate open, leave it that way. Livestock may need it open to get access to water or to the barn, come milking time. Likewise, all gates that are closed must be closed again once you've passed through. And always wait up for the person who is handling the gates; if you move off before that person is ready, his horse will want to follow your horse. Closing a gate and battling a horse at the same time is no fun.

ON THE TRAIL

When on an organized trail ride, never ride ahead of the recognized trail boss. If no such person is appointed, make certain your group sticks to clearly marked trails and that someone not involved in the ride knows where you plan to ride. Someone in the group must carry first aid and emergency supplies for both humans and horses, no matter how short the planned outing. Such a kit should include a canteen of water, a swatch of clean cotton cloth, bandages and wraps, aspirin, phenylbutazone (bute) tablets, a chemical ice pack, insect repellent, waterproof matches, a stout halter and tie rope and a flashlight. Also take along a warm blanket or sweater and some food in the event you have to spend an unplanned night out of doors. You don't have to be far from civilization to suffer real privation if an emergency catches you unawares.

When trail riding, keep the pace and level of difficulty of the ride appropriate to the least able horse-and-rider team. Teaming up with horses and riders of similar abilities will help you avoid unhappy situations. If a large group goes out with several riders more experienced than the group as a whole, consider splitting up for a while and rejoining at a designated time and place. This allows everyone to have a good time without endangering the person on a green horse or the rider with less ability. On the other hand, as a kindness you might decide to ride your experienced mount along with that green horse or rider.

Whenever you ride out with a group, regardless of the general level of experience, stay aware of what's going on around you. Drinking and horseback riding don't mix. On a formal ride, if you find yourself riding along with one or more drinking people, do yourself and your horse a favor and move on to another group at the first safe opportunity. If the drinking and/or riding and tomfoolery appear to be getting out of hand, a quiet word to the trail boss might be in order.

When tying horses out on the trail, avoid tying them to mature trees. Horses like eating the bark from trees, and saplings offer less to chew on. Your tie rope can also damage bark. If you camp or stop to eat more than once in any given spot, move your horse around so he doesn't overtrample the vegetation surrounding a particular tree. Make certain that supplies taken into the woods or wilderness are taken back out. Few things are more distressing to the nature lover than discarded beer cans and candy wrappers littering the scenery in the middle of nowhere.

ROAD RIDING

When riding on the road, ride single file. If there's a green or nervous horse along and you're on a steady animal, ride a safe distance behind and slightly to the outside of the youngster. If your horse will tolerate it, ride ahead of the problem horse, with that horse's muzzle as close to your animal's inside hip as possible. Your horse's calmness will almost certainly be transferred to the nervous horse. Riding in either of these two positions will allow you to signal drivers to slow down by holding your hand out and down, palm side facing rearward. If the other horse panics, your horse can pull up alongside or stop, to bar him from whirling out in front of traffic.

If a rider anticipates this sort of reaction and roads can't be avoided, plan to pony the troublesome horse. Attach a long lead line to his halter and lead him from the back of your horse. Make certain, if you plan to

Avoid riding your horse on roads until he is well accustomed to all kinds of traffic.

ride shotgun this way, that your horse is steady, sturdy and obedient, and that the two horses have been taught to get along. You must be confident of your ability to handle any situation. If a nervous and/or green horse is along, it's best to avoid road riding altogether, at least until the animal is somewhat tired.

SOLITARY TRAIL RIDING

If you like solitary trail riding, make your outings as safe as possible. In this case it's doubly important that you tell someone where you plan to ride and when to expect you back. Stick to safe, familiar trails; save trailblazing for a time when you're with a friend or two. Carry emergency medical supplies. And just as when you're swimming, pace yourself. Don't go out so far that you'll have difficulty getting back before dark or before your horse suffers exhaustion. Never ride alone in an area known to be inhabited by bears or other dangerous wildlife, or on a horse that tends to spook hard at deer, squirrels, rabbits and rustling leaves.

ARENA RULES

Arena riding comes with its own set of rules. When riding in an arena, always ride at a similar speed and in the same direction as the other horses. If you must pass a horse, move over into the inside lane (farthest from the rail) and signal your intent to the other rider by saying "pass, please!" As always, keep a safe distance away from the other horse as you pass. Move back onto the rail as soon as you've passed the other horse. Never show off, and avoid riding close to anyone else who does. Enter and leave the arena at whatever gait and speed the judge indicates.

At horse shows, stay out of the ring except during your scheduled classes. More than one embarrassed rider has attempted a short cut across the ring, only to find himself in the middle of an unscheduled class. Accustom your horse to the show ring and arena riding prior to the show, even if it means staying overnight and paying to use the facilities of a local stable.

Outfit yourself and your horse with apparel and tack appropriate for the events in which you plan to compete, and buy the best quality you can afford. Ride only in classes suitable to your abilities and those of your horse. Competing too far over your head will result in discouragement, and deliberately competing in classes for which you are overqualified is taking unfair advantage of other competitors. But once you've gotten a taste for competition, don't be afraid to challenge yourself and your horse.

When observing other competitors from outside the ring, keep a 6- to 8-foot distance between yourself and the arena rail, farther away if you are astride your horse. If you stand any closer, you may distract a competitor's horse. Avoid littering the showgrounds, and pick up any papers and cans you see lying around. A carelessly tossed food wrapper skittering in the wind may cause a horse to shy and throw his rider.

When circumstances dictate that another pet come along to the show grounds, keep it on a leash at all times. While it's perfectly all right to bring children along, make certain they know how to behave properly, and safely, around horses.

At a show, maintain a safe distance between horses, and stay on the rail. Enter and leave the arena in orderly fashion. Spectators should avoid hanging on or leaning too close to the rail.

If you lunge your horse at the show grounds, do so in a clear, safe place. If you tie your horse, make certain he can't get loose and that he is tied safely. Be considerate of your mount: Make sure he gets plenty of rest, and water, between classes, and don't schedule him for so many classes that he is overtaxed.

AT AUCTION

The auction arena presents another set of rules. The first is that spectators should stay out of the arena at all times. No matter how many "wheeler dealers" are in the arena, or how great the temptation is to get in there for a better look, or to let others get a better look at you—stay out! Bystanders in the auction arena block the view of other participants, and place themselves and auction exhibitors at risk.

Make absolutely certain you want the particular horse you're planning to bid on. At almost every country or county horse auction, all sales are final. When the gavel goes down, you've bought that horse. If the animal starts limping as you lead him out of the arena, then you've bought that limp. Buying horses this way is risky at best, foolhardy at worst. Reneging on an auction purchase is wrong—so you'd better know what you're getting into before bidding.

GET IT IN WRITING

Whether you are buying, selling, leasing, boarding or transporting, you should put in writing any agreements you make regarding a horse. When you purchase a horse, get a clearly written, signed and dated bill of sale. If the animal is registered, make certain all papers are in order. Provide a bill of sale and all necessary paperwork for anyone purchasing a horse from you. While it's true most good business can be done on a handshake, the best deals are also sealed with a signature.

Always endeavor to be honest and gracious. There will be other rides, other shows, other sales. But there's never a more opportune time than the present to do or say the right thing.

Twelve

DEALING WITH
COMMON VICES

*A*nyone who spends time with horses is eventually confronted by some equine's unacceptable habit. Fortunately, most of the bad habits horses develop can be eliminated or minimized (although a few cannot). Still others require the services of a professional horse handler. Again, no two horses are alike: A habit from which one horse is easily dissuaded may prove to be an incurable vice in another animal.

It's important to remember that there's no such thing as a "cookie cutter" horse, and shouldn't be. All horses are different, and none are perfect in every regard. We need to respect this fact when dealing with any given horse, and appreciate the animal's good qualities and learn to accommodate him at certain times. We shouldn't consistently allow an animal to get away with inappropriate behavior, but sometimes a good horse who can't be convinced to give up a bad habit deserves to be accommodated.

I own a wonderful Quarter Horse gelding, for example, who does it all. Champ is excellent on the trail, safe for beginners to ride, flashy and obedient in the show ring and a real pal to work around. This book, in fact, is dedicated to that horse. But as good as he is, he is not perfect. He absolutely refuses to tie hard and fast. No matter what we try, he will intermittently, and vigorously, test anything to which he is tethered.

Rather than risk the horse injuring himself or bystanders, we simply never tie him. We've taught him to ground tie, which he will do for hours at a time. When this isn't enough, we use a portable corral, which he respects like a gentleman.

Another mare in our small herd becomes so easily attached to other horses that every time I take her out by herself, she needs to be reweaned from her friends. I can ride that horse for one hour with an animal she's never seen before, and by the end of that hour, she'll cry out for the other horse when we separate. I've worked so much with the mare that she now considers me her closest herd mate, so I can and do ride her out by herself. But if I didn't have the time to form this kind of bond, I'd simply choose another horse for solitary trail riding, and ride her only with friends. It would be more enjoyable for both the horse and myself. Also, if I could own only one horse, it would not be this mare. She is the type of horse that craves some equine companionship.

Some people might call these tactics "spoiling" the horse. I call it being sensitive to the temperament and needs of various horses. It is only humane, and realistic, to make an occasional accommodation.

BAD HABITS: ENVIRONMENTAL

Domesticated horses are largely subject to conditions far different from those nature intended. The more unnatural the horse's living conditions, the more likely he is to develop bad habits as compensation. This is one good argument for keeping horses in as natural a state as possible, with plenty of turnout, exercise and food to graze on. It is far easier to prevent a bad habit from developing than it is to eliminate one after it's become ingrained.

Cribbing and Windsucking

Cribbing is a case in point. A horse that cribs will grab with his teeth onto a solid object, such as a stall divider or the edge of an empty feeder, pull his muzzle toward his chest, arch his neck and gulp air. Cribbing usually results from an animal becoming bored and having too little access to bulk food. His grazing nature causes him to crave oral stimulation and a feeling of fullness, while his environment prevents him from satisfying these desires. To pass the long, lonely, hungry hours in his stall, he creates his own oral stimulation with whatever is at hand and fills his gut up with air. Very intelligent animals can learn to do this without so much as a board to bite onto; they bite onto their own tongues, arch their necks, and suck down air. This habit is called windsucking.

Both cribbing and windsucking disturb an animal's digestion and may lead to colic. Cribbing is such a pernicious habit that cribbers may prefer board sucking to eating. This may result in extreme unthriftiness (high caloric needs), so that some cribbers, no matter how well managed and fed, are in poor rig (condition).

These are impossible habits to break. The most the owner of a cribber or windsucker can hope for is that an artificial neck device, called a cribbing strap, will prevent the animal from being able to arch his neck and thus suck in wind. While a cure is highly unlikely, the prevention or modification of these habits is simple: Offer plenty of free-choice hay or pasture, and turn the horse out every day, preferably with herd mates. If a horse must be kept confined, he should be offered free-choice hay. Regular grooming and riding are also musts for the confined horse.

Weaving and Stall Walking

Like cribbing and windsucking, weaving and stall walking are vices created as a response to boredom. Horses that weave stand in one spot and weave their heads from side to side while shifting their weight from one side to another. Stall walkers pace the edges of their stalls, from one end to another almost continually. Stallions, who are often kept continually confined to prevent unwanted access to mares, are noted for these habits. Besides making the animal unthrifty, these habits place heavy stress on their joints, particularly the legs, and can lead to early arthritis and breakdown. Only the owner of an animal with one of these vices can tell you how nerve-racking it is to have a weaver or stall walker in the barn; it's somewhat like owning an animal that's possessed!

Once again, there's no real cure for these habits, though they may be modified. Both prevention and modification lie in giving the animal plenty of exercise, attention and turnout.

Wood Chewing

Wood chewing is a habit that can be costly for both horse and owner. I once bought a gelding that chewed through a 2-inch by 6-inch rail the first night he was placed in his new stall. Such behavior is bad for the horse's digestion, will ruin his teeth and over time will cost his owner a fortune. Unpalatable commercial preparations that discourage a horse from chewing wood can be painted on all exposed surfaces. A home-made "chew stop" recipe consists of several cloves of garlic and ½ cup of hot pepper sauce mixed with a quart of liquid vegetable oil. Simmer this mixture for an hour, then paint it over exposed wood. This is how I handled the situation with the aforementioned gelding, but with limited results, at least for the first week. Though the gelding quit chewing the treated wood, he kept coming up with new alternatives, such as chewing his feeder and wall supports. His wood chewing ceased altogether, however, once we started turning him out with the other horses every day.

Stall Kicking and Pawing

Stall kicking is another habit that will destroy your barn. If too long confined, an energetic horse will take out his frustrations on the walls of his stall. Or he may become frightened at something, such as a snake or rodent, and kick at his stall dividers in an effort to escape the perceived danger. If he manages to escape, then his behavior is rewarded by freedom. A bad habit is born.

Horses that continually paw at the floors of their stalls are also exhibiting frustrated energy. Pawing results in damage to the animal's front legs and feet. A pawing horse's stall floors are nearly impossible to maintain.

Some people attach short, heavy chains to the front pasterns of a pawing horse, or the back pasterns of a stall kicker. A 6-inch length of 2- by 4-inch lumber, firmly attached by a soft cotton rope, can also be used. When a horse starts pawing or kicking, the chain or wood swings back and hits him hard in the pastern. If you own a horse that kicks or paws, you may have to use such a device, but reserve it as a last resort. First, see that your horse gets plenty of exercise and turnout. If the animal is already turned out most of the time, it's possible he just needs to learn patience (see Chapter Ten). One mare I owned grew impatient only when she knew I was going to open her stall door and allow her to run out to pasture. As soon as another horse went out, she would begin pawing frantically and trying to rush the gate. To cure her of these antics, I started leading her outside and tying her to a fence post for a half hour or so. As soon as she stopped associating turnout with instant freedom, she started behaving herself.

In any event, stall walls should be sturdy enough to withstand kicking—¼" plywood won't do. Your best bet is 2- by 6-inch hardwood planking. A horse that kicks through the wall will do more permanent damage to his legs than he does to the barn. Minimize the damage to a stall floor of a pawing horse by installing a wood and gravel base, as described in Chapter Four.

HEREDITY VS. ENVIRONMENT

I've heard experienced horsemen claim that bad habits are contagious, that they are learned behavior picked up from other animals, and that the tendency to form such habits is inherited. These people refuse to add a cribber or weaver to their herd, and decline to breed such animals. It's true some horses are more temperamentally prone to picking up bad habits. They are more sensitive, intelligent, energetic and/or given to boredom than the average horse. Such an animal may, indeed, learn compensatory behavior for environmental deprivation by watching other horses.

This is especially true in the case of a dam and foal. The foal inherits the same intelligence and tendency to boredom as his dam. By watching his mother, he learns to mimic the behavior that's become her compensation. The breeder assumes the foal directly inherited the behavior from his dam. The foal actually acquired the habit thanks to the breeder, who failed to provide the little guy with a naturally satisfying environment.

I firmly believe that most of the bad habits so far mentioned are developed as the result of poor horse management. Most horses exhibiting these behaviors aren't bad by nature; in fact they are often the most highly intelligent, creative, sensitive and energetic of animals. Ironically, it is our best horses that are most likely to be damaged or destroyed by mismanagement. Regrettably, such mismanagement, especially at large commercial horse establishments, is often the norm rather than the exception.

VICES: ON THE GROUND

There are some procedures we subject our horses to that, while unnatural, are nevertheless necessary. We need to tie our horses, to catch them, lead them, load them on trailers, haul them to various places, feed them at times convenient to us and handle their feet and mouths. Some horses refuse to adapt to these domestic requirements or rebel against one or more of these procedures at some point. Then it falls to us, for the horse's sake as well as our own, to teach such an animal to quietly accept its lot in life.

Refusal to Tie

An animal that won't tie is called a halter puller. Such a horse, though he may be as quiet and obedient as a pussy cat at other times, turns into a crazy creature the instant someone tries to tie him to a stationary object. He rears up and then violently throws all his weight back against the restraint in an effort to be free of it. Because horses are so powerful, it takes some real forethought to prevent a halter puller from obtaining his goal of breaking free.

Halter pulling may result from an animal being badly frightened, or even beaten, while he was tied. The threat could have been real or merely perceived. It's possible that the person who first taught the horse to tie did a poor job of it. Whatever the original cause, once a horse succeeds in breaking loose once or twice, he begins to test everything he's tied to, and the habit quickly becomes firmly entrenched. Make a point of not allowing your horse to ever get into this habit in the first place. Whenever you tie your horse, use extra sturdy nylon halters, heavy ropes and bull snaps that are firmly tied into the rope. Also make certain the horse is tied to something so stout it will withstand every effort to break free.

If you own a confirmed halter puller, resign yourself to the fact that this horse will always try to break free, and tie him accordingly. Another way to handle the confirmed halter puller is to teach him to hobble and ground tie, and restrain him only in a corral or pen whenever these restraints aren't feasible. In the long run, this management system is probably the safest alternative, as tied halter pullers are always dangerous. There's no telling when such a horse will suddenly rear up and set back violently. Anyone standing to the front of or too close behind such an animal is in serious danger. It's hardly practical to expect you'll have a chance to warn everyone who might ever inadvertently walk around your tied horse that he's dangerous.

You also might try using a belly rope (see page 127) or a Be Nice halter on such an animal. The Be Nice halter is specially designed to exert pressure on the poll whenever a horse sets back. The pressure is relieved when the horse stops resisting his restraint. Most horses, once they've become accustomed to this halter, will not pull back so long as

164

You need both "bait" (grain) and "hook" (halter and lead rope) to catch a horse at pasture. This young horse is so eager for a bite of grain that he ignores the halter and lead rope.

they are tied with it. It's a device worth trying, but be aware some horses go literally wild the first time such a halter takes hold at the poll. This can result in injury and further psychological trauma to the horse, so have a sharp knife on hand to cut the animal loose should trouble develop.

The Hard to Catch Horse

Horses who are caught only when they're to be put to work are likely to develop the habit of evading capture. Who can blame them?

Usually this problem can be solved by teaching the horse that being caught is a nonthreatening, even enjoyable, experience. Though the remedy takes some time, it is well worth the effort. Few things are more irritating than going out to catch your horse for the big show or trail ride, only to have him evade you for so long that it becomes too late to go.

You can't catch fish without bait and a hook. Likewise, you need to be prepared to "bait and hook" your horse when you bring him in from the pasture. When you feed your horse his daily grain ration, make a habit of placing the feed in a metal bucket and shaking the bucket so the feed rattles against the sides. This creates a sound the horse soon learns to associate with food. Once your horse has made that association, go out to the pasture once or twice a day with a small bucket of sweet grain in one hand (bait), and a lead rope and halter in the other (hook). Determinedly aim toward your horse. Avoid chasing him, but no matter how much he tries to evade you, don't quit walking toward his shoulder. As you walk, rattle the grain in the bucket and talk to him. Eventually he'll realize you aren't going to give up and that you've got something good to eat anyway. The first few times he finally stops evading you to eat, simply stand and allow him to do so. Give him a pat and kind word and leave the pasture after he's cleaned up the grain. No matter how tempting, do not under any circumstances put the halter and lead on and take him back to the barn to work. This will totally destroy any further chances of reform.

After he easily allows you to approach him with the grain bucket, slip the lead rope over his neck and place his halter on before allowing him to eat the grain (horses should never be put out to pasture with halters on, as they can get them caught on fences, branches or their own feet and be seriously injured). Once the horse has eaten the grain, lead him around for a minute, while enjoying some pleasant conversation. Now remove the halter and lead, and let the horse go. After a week or so of this, your horse will be easy to catch. He'll probably come running to the barn as soon as you call his name and rattle the grain bucket.

This behavior won't last, however, if you revert back to working the horse every time he's caught. Make a habit of going out once or twice a week to catch him just for a little treat and a visit. If you always carry a lead and halter, he won't know if you're planning to bring him in to work or if you're just coming out to enjoy his company.

Biting and Kicking

If your horse is the kind that threatens to bite or, worse, kick when you approach him in his pasture or stall, carry a lungeing or dressage whip whenever you go into his territory. Chances are that if you carry it you won't need to use it, but still exercise caution. I once owned a gelding that was extremely territorial. He threatened to attack anyone coming into his pasture. No matter how careful you are around such an animal, one day he's going to succeed in injuring you or some other unsuspecting person. My best advice for the owner of such a horse is, no matter how well behaved he might be under saddle, get rid of him before someone is seriously injured.

Feeding Time Meanness

Some horses are mean only at feeding time, or at least they make a great pretense of meanness by pinning back their ears and threatening to bite. This is a common vice, brought on largely by our need to feed only at certain times of the day, which makes some horses frantic. Using the threat of a whip, teach such a horse to stand well back in his stall while you fill his manger or grain bucket. Then simply leave him alone until he's finished eating.

This brings up another point: Nearly all domestic horses are territorial about their food. A dominant horse will do its best to prevent less-aggressive animals from eating anything put out to the herd at large. For this reason, if you feed hay outdoors, arrange it in several feeders or tubs scattered over a wide area. If a less dominant animal is pushed away from one feed station, he can move over to another. If you feed grain to more than one horse, you must separate them completely before offering grain rations. The best practice is to bring each horse into its own stall and feed grain from there. Horses never consider grain to be community property.

Bolting Feed

Some horses bolt their grain, which can lead to colic or, at the least, poor digestion of expensive feed. To combat this habit, place several large rocks (they must be at least three inches in diameter to prevent accidental ingestion) in the horse's manger or grain bucket. He'll have to pick his grain from around the rocks, which will slow him down.

Hard to Handle Feet

Though all horses instinctively resist having their feet and mouths handled, some are more resistant than others. It is up to us to slowly but surely accustom our horses to accept routine handling of their feet and mouths.

To handle the feet of a horse, follow the procedure outlined in Chapter Five. When working on the horse's foot, be careful not to dig too deeply into the sensitive cleft around the frog. Set the foot down carefully, rather than dropping it painfully on the toe. Always work around the horse in the same sequence, so he can calmly anticipate your next move.

For a horse that's already become rebellious about foot handling, bribery works very well. I own a mare that had a reputation, when I purchased her, of being impossible to shoe. She fought and kicked out wildly, especially when asked for a back foot. When we tried to lift a front foot, she fell to the ground. Careful examination of her front pasterns revealed old rope-burn scars, an indication that she'd been previously thrown down to be shod. This was in keeping with the kind of treatment I knew she'd endured under her previous owner. Being thrown off its feet is a terrifying experience for any horse. I had to overcome that terror and teach this mare to trust not only me but anyone else who might need to handle her feet in the future.

I started with my young daughter as assistant. In her own safe stall, without restraint except for a halter and lead rope, I instructed my daughter to offer grain each time I asked for the mare's foot. So long as she complied and allowed me to first lean into her and touch firmly, and then pick up and hold her foot, she was permitted to eat. Whenever she withdrew the foot, my daughter withdrew the grain. After she allowed me to handle each foot for even a few seconds, her first lesson was over. Within a week, I could pick up all four feet and work on them without trouble. The first time my farrier came to work on this horse, we shod only her front feet. We did so while her closest herd mate was close by; we took our time and asked her to balance on three feet for only short periods. Again I offered treats for good behavior. There was no yelling or hitting, nothing to awaken the old terror. A week later, we were able to put shoes on her back feet. This innately kind horse, who had a reputation as a real rogue, was totally accepting of any treatment involving her feet in less than two weeks.

Hard to Handle Mouth

From time to time you or someone else will need to examine your horse's mouth for proper fitting of a bit, for sores or for sharp teeth or otherwise painful tooth configurations. Someone interested in purchasing your horse may want to check his teeth for age. Geldings often need to have their wolf teeth pulled, and young horses sometimes suffer impacted baby teeth, which require extraction. For these reasons, it is important that your horse allow routine handling of his mouth.

Handling the mouth can be dangerous, as an animal that rears up in protest may prove lethal. Start this work slowly, and start work standing in close to the horse's left side. Never move directly in front of the horse unless he's submitting quietly, and even then remain cautious.

The halter must have plenty of room at the noseband, so as not to restrict motion of the mouth. Work quietly and calmly, and use only as much restraint as necessary. Some horses require nothing more than a halter and lead rope; others may need a twitch. Horses that violently resist may have to be tranquilized before it's safe to examine their mouths. Though many practitioners routinely use a speculum to open a horse's mouth, most horses violently resist this large, heavy piece of metal, which can be dangerous to horse and human when used on a resistant animal. It's far better to accustom your horse to simple handling of his mouth.

Start at the left side of the horse, standing close. Slip your index and middle fingers into the horse's mouth at the bars, just as you would if you were asking the horse to open up for a bit. If you're working with a stallion or gelding, be careful not to gouge yourself on a sharp canine tooth. You may want to wear rubber gloves, both as protection and in order to more firmly grasp the horse's tongue.

Then slip your thumb into the same space, beneath your index and middle fingers, and gently grasp the horse's tongue. Pull it out the side of his mouth. If he's submitting quietly, step in front of the horse while holding the tongue outside his mouth, and take a good look inside. Once you've examined the front teeth and those at the right rear of the horse's mouth, gently move the tongue around until you're holding it out the right side of the horse's mouth. Now you can examine the teeth on the left side of his jaw.

Pushy on the Lead Line

Some horses are very uncivilized when being led. They push into the handler, stepping on toes, or pull ahead or back, or lag behind. If you have such problems, go over the basic leading training with your horse, as described in Chapter Ten. Though you ought to wear sturdy leather footwear whenever working with horses, it becomes doubly important that you do so when working with a pushy horse. Safety-toed boots might even be in order.

Make certain that whenever you lead a horse through a gate or doorway, there's plenty of room for the two of you to pass through side by side. A horse that's afraid of banging its hip on a doorway or gate will push toward you out of self protection. If the passageway is too narrow for you to walk through together, then ask your horse to stand, pass through yourself, turn to face the horse, move to one side so that he won't jump on you, then ask him to walk through.

Refusal to Load

Horse trailers are a horror to most horses. Some quickly overcome their instinctive fear of entering a narrow, confining dark place. Others need more convincing. To train a horse to load requires great patience, perseverance and not a few outright tricks.

The easiest method for training a horse to load is one where you keep an open trailer out where horses have continual access to it. Give the animal being trained his daily grain ration on the trailer. Start by walking the horse up to the back of the trailer and letting him eat from a bucket there. Then move onto the trailer (if there's an escape hatch) and let him have his grain only while his two front feet are up on the trailer. If there is no escape hatch door, snap a long rope or lunge line to the horse's halter, and bring the free end through the trailer and out the escape window or hatch. Place the grain bucket up on the trailer. As the horse steps toward the grain, take up the slack rope, but do not tug or pull the horse forward or he will almost surely resist. As training progresses, move the grain back farther and farther, until the horse's entire body is on the trailer.

Once he's enticed all the way into the trailer, leave the back door open while he eats. When he's more at ease, close the door and latch the butt bar and leave him on a few minutes after he's finished his meal. The next step is to take him for a ride around the block; a haynet full of hay for this first trip and perhaps a calm companion horse who is already accustomed to hauling should help pacify his nerves. Make certain his head is tied, but leave about 14 inches of rope so the horse can move his head from side to side and lower it for comfort.

Try to accustom your horse to being loaded and hauled before it becomes necessary. Trying to force a nervous horse to jump on a trailer in time for the big show is asking for trouble. If you don't own a trailer, then rent or borrow one for a few days prior to needing it. Or rig up a wooden step-up box that will approximate the feeling of a trailer for your horse, and use that for training.

If your horse is a real problem loader, there are several tricks you can try. Make certain before starting any loading retraining that you have plenty of time to finish the training. If the horse gets away with refusal to load, you will have reinforced this bad habit. Always wear gloves during these sessions, to avoid the real possibility of suffering rope burn.

The first thing to try is loading an experienced, calm pasture mate onto the trailer. Your horse might just surprise you and jump right on in order to be with his friend. Or park the trailer where a gate can be opened to create a sort of loading chute. Run a long length of heavy cotton rope from the front tie of the trailer, out behind the horse under the tail (don't allow it to droop so much that he can tangle his back legs in it) and back through the trailer to your hand. Now, using grain, sweet talk and intermittent pressure on the rope, encourage the horse to walk forward. Once he has loaded, reward him liberally. If he pulls back off the trailer before you close the doors, repeat the lesson until he goes on and stays on.

If, in fact, the horse continues to pull off before getting all the way on, or right after getting on but before being closed in, you'll need to teach him another lesson. When the horse tries to pull back, stand outside the trailer with the long lead rope in one hand and a lungeing whip in the other and swat the horse's hind legs beneath the hocks. You can even use this method to get the horse loaded.

Though it's good to have assistance with these lessons, it's possible to use ropes and a lungeing whip to load a reluctant horse—and keep him loaded—all by yourself. Sometimes the more people you have stamping and hollering, the more upset, frightened and stubborn the horse becomes. Simply put, the horse needs to learn only that it's more pleasant to go onto the trailer than it is to resist going onto the trailer. You'll need to use as much force and/or ingenuity as it takes to convince him of this, which may be considerable. Try to keep these lessons as matter of fact as possible, keep your goals in mind and, no matter what, hang onto your temper.

Refusal to Lunge

A horse that refuses to lunge has either been spoiled by an inexperienced handler at the other end of the line or frightened by the lungeing whip. Whatever the case, you must overcome his reluctance and teach him to keep forward movement on the lunge line. Lungeing is far too valuable a tool to give up, to say nothing of the lesson in respect your horse will learn once you've taught him to obey you on the line.

Lungeing is usually easy, so long as you follow the instructions given in Chapter Ten. Remember to use body language to force the horse forward or to ask him to slow down or stop. Use the lungeing whip consistently to reinforce your body and voice commands. Reward the horse for obedience, keep on him for disobedience. Stay sharp, so you can read when the horse plans to rebel and act instantaneously to prevent it. Usually it's that simple.

I once dealt with a horse, however, that was a real challenge, both on the lunge line and off. On the lunge line, he raced around like a mad thing. If I stepped forward toward his shoulder in an effort to make him slow down or stop, he reared up, whirled and raced around in the other direction. The first few times I worked him on the line, he tried to rear up and strike, and even the lungeing whip hardly dissuaded him from attack. After working with this horse for weeks, as a desperate last resort I taught him to submit to a bitting rig and lunged him in that (this is usually not recommended, as a horse who rears in a bitting rig may flip over backward). Before long I was able to lunge him this way quite successfully. But then he discovered a new trick: he moved in closer and closer to me on the circle. Twice I was careless and he managed to sneak in close enough to kick me. Though this gelding was extraordinarily good-looking, had a kind eye and seemed quiet, he was totally unpredictable. Whenever I started to think I could trust him, he'd pull some dirty trick.

How did I finally solve this problem? I didn't. I traded the horse to a more experienced handler (who eventually sold him to a meat buyer at auction).

The point I want to make is an important one: Though most training problems can be solved with patience and persistence, a few cannot. When dealing with spoiled horses, always recognize your limitations and act accordingly.

PROBLEMS UNDER SADDLE

If you ride long enough, you're likely to run into a horse that has one or more bad habits under saddle. It's not our aim to teach anyone how to become a bronc rider (and such a thing can hardly be taught in a book, in any case). Never hesitate to seek professional help if it seems that a horse's problem is more than you can safely handle. While there are problems that can be handled at home, there are other times when a horse's behavior demands the immediate attention of a professional trainer.

A vice that is dangerous to handle in one horse may be little more than a nuisance in another. You must judge for yourself what you feel you can deal with. If you're nervous and uncertain, always err on the side of caution.

Bridle Shy

A bridle-shy horse is one that resists the bit and/or bridle. Often this problem originates because someone hurt the horse's teeth when inserting or taking out the bit or twisted his sensitive ear or scraped his eye with a strap or browband. To further complicate matters, when a horse begins to resist out of pain and fear, an insensitive handler may become more and more rough, thus inflicting more pain and creating greater resistance. To overcome the effects of such handling, the horse must learn to trust you.

The first rule is: Inflict no pain. Under no circumstances should you jam the bit against the horse's front teeth in an effort to get him to open his mouth. Handle the bridle straps carefully. Take your time.

When a horse lifts his head and clamps his jaw to resist the bit, you need to keep the horse's head down, within reach. To do this, leave a halter on the horse, and tie him in cross-ties short enough that he can't get his head into the upper stratosphere—but not so tight that he can't move his head at all; otherwise he may panic.

To start retraining, use a simple bridle with no more straps than necessary. To start, one with a browband, simple snaffle or curb bit and curb strap is enough. The curb strap should be unhooked so it can't catch on the horse's lower jaw. Put some jam, honey or molasses on the bit. Stand close on the horse's near (left) side at the shoulder, facing forward. Hold the bridle with the crown piece in your right hand, the bit

A bridle-shy horse will throw his head and clamp his jaws to resist bridling.

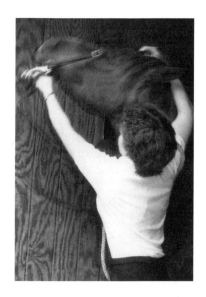

This horse is encouraged to keep his head in the lower stratosphere by the handler's arm over his poll and a rope over his neck, which offers the handler extra control, should she need it. Bridling over a halter with the horse standing in cross-ties will serve the same purpose. Make sure the horse doesn't panic and resist the cross-ties. The handler slips a thumb into the bar area of the mouth to encourage the horse to open up. She is extra careful not to bang the bit against the horse's teeth, or hurt his eyes or ears with the bridle straps. Even very resistant horses often succumb to the allure of jam or molasses on the bit.

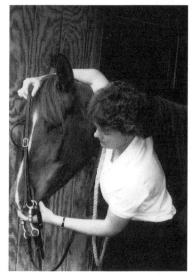

in your left. Holding the bridle in position in front of the horse, insert your thumb into the space at the bars in the horse's mouth. Wiggle it around or press down on the tongue until the horse opens his mouth. Then insert the bit while sliding the crown piece (carefully) up and then over the horse's ears. If the horse still resists, try unbuckling the cheek

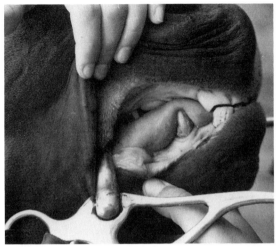

Stallions and geldings have wolf teeth that may interfere with the action of the bit and eventually cause pain. If a male horse is bridle-shy or tosses his head when under saddle, check to make certain his wolf teeth aren't being banged by the bit. If so, try another bit, arrange to have the teeth pulled or ride with a bitless bridle, such as a hackamore.

straps, and rebuckle them after the bridle is on. This method is easier on the horse's ears, which may be the cause of the resistance. Putting something sweet on the bit will have your horse gobbling the bit up in no time.

To avoid further problems, check to make sure the bit and bridle are in good condition, are a good fit and are properly adjusted. A rusty, pitted bit is good for nothing but the junk pile. Once in the mouth, there should be about ¼" clearance on each side. If the bit is jointed at the corners, make certain it doesn't pinch the horse's mouth when the reins are pulled. If it does, attach rubber bit guards. I have one walking horse with such thin skin at the corners of her mouth that even soft rubber bit guards rub sores on her face. For such an animal, you may have to use a different style of bit altogether.

When adjusting the bridle, pull it just tight enough so there's a slight wrinkle at each corner of the mouth. The curb strap or chain should be loose enough to allow you to insert two fingers sideways between it and the horse's lower jaw. When the reins are pulled back, the curb strap should not pull so severely that the horse appears to be grinning or is forced to open its mouth for relief.

It helps if you keep the horse's bridle path clipped short, as mane hairs can easily get twisted in the bridle. In addition to causing discomfort, too much soft, bulky mane at the crown makes it difficult to adjust the bridle for good action.

Balks at Being Cinched

A horse that kicks out, snaps or blows up its belly (or just blows up) when the cinch is pulled tight has probably suffered a bad experience. To overcome these problems, use a well-padded cinch or girth strap. Pull it up at first only enough to hold the saddle in place. Now walk the horse around, pulling the cinch a little tighter every minute or so until it's properly adjusted. This doesn't mean to cut the horse nearly in two. You should balance well enough in the saddle to ride with a cinch that's pulled only moderately tight. Once the cinch is as tight as necessary, stand in front of the horse and pull each front leg slowly forward from the knee. This ensures that the girth isn't tightened over wrinkled skin, which may cause a gall.

Refuses to Stand for Mounting

A horse that refuses to stand still while you mount is worse than a nuisance; he can be downright dangerous. To teach a horse to stand, have an assistant stand at the horse's head and hold him while you mount up. If the horse moves while your foot is in the stirrup, immediately drop the foot down, reprimand the animal and start over. You must not complete mounting while the horse is moving. Once the horse is standing still for mounting, position him at a fence or corral corner. Ask your assistant to stand a few feet away from the horse's head on his open side while you practice mounting on your own. If the horse moves, the assistant quickly moves in to reinforce the notion that he must stand still. As the horse learns to stand still while you mount, move him farther and farther away from the fence until you can mount him standing still by himself in the open. This lesson may need to be reinforced once or twice, but it usually won't take many sessions to retrain an animal with this vice.

If you have no one to help you, then you'll have to use another method. In this case, bridle your horse over his halter. Take him to a fence or corral corner, and tie him using a heavy rope and snap attached to his halter ring. Put your foot in the stirrup. Pull your foot out of the stirrup and reprimand the horse each time he moves. Practice mounting this way until the horse stands still while you mount completely. Now dismount and unhook the tie snap and practice mounting without it. Gradually move the horse so you're working farther and farther away from the fence. The first time he stands still in the open and lets you mount, praise him lavishly and move on to more relaxing work.

To avoid this problem, never let your horse move off until after you've mounted and made him stand still for half a minute or so. Also, be careful to settle lightly in the saddle, push your boot toe firmly into the girth to avoid kicking him in the ribs as you swing up and be careful never to pull on the reins, which will cause the bit to jab his mouth as you mount.

BALKING, JIGGING AND BOLTING

A horse that refuses to move forward at your command is balking. Balking takes many forms, from a horse that rears to one that bucks to the old sluggard who merely plants all four feet firmly on the ground and says "no sir!" Whether or not you can handle a balker depends on your riding skill, your patience and the form your horse's balking takes.

The Balking Horse

If your horse simply refuses to move forward, use whatever means necessary to get him moving; a riding crop behind the leg is a good motivator. So are spurs, but don't use them unless your leg position and balance are stable enough that you don't inadvertently poke the horse with your spurs as you ride. Such skill takes considerable time and experience to develop.

If the horse succeeds at not moving forward, the next step is often backing up—and the step after that is rearing. Insist at all times that your horse move forward when you say so. A horse that's gotten away with balking may require one or two real confrontations before changing his mind for the better. If this is the case with your horse, don't hesitate to hire a professional or to ask a very good rider to handle the horse for you once or twice, just to get him settled down before you take over the reins. However, don't expect that another rider will be able to do all the work for you. Many horses, especially those that have been spoiled at one time, will test every rider to see what they can get away with. Keep someone on hand to help the first time you work the horse yourself, and be prepared to be firm.

Often the reason horses balk is that they don't want to leave the barnyard; this is called being barn sour. And though it's good for a horse to be regularly turned out with other horses, this can also create a problem. Some horses become herd bound, that is, so attached to herd mates that they resist riding away from them. Other horses, though they can be convinced to leave home, try to run back, or bolt, the minute their noses are turned in that direction. A jigging horse sort of prances on its toes, usually as a result of nervousness or anticipation at going home.

Most horses, if not used regularly, develop some degree of attachment to the herd and/or the barn, and demonstrate one or more of the above habits. If yours is sour or has any other of the bad habits related to balking, your best bet is to institute a logical, progressive retraining plan before attempting any pleasure riding.

Rearing

If your horse rears, get off at the first safe moment and put the animal in the hands of a professional trainer, or get rid of it. Rearing is a deadly vice no amateur should ever attempt to handle. A horse that rears up far enough can flip over backward onto his rider.

A rearing horse is dangerous. Avoid riding such an animal, if at all possible.

If you unexpectedly find yourself on a rearer, force the horse into tight circles when its front feet hit the ground. As soon as it seems safe to do so, stop and dismount.

If you should find yourself unexpectedly on a rearing horse, lean far forward, clutching the horse's mane for security, if need be. When the horse comes down, grab one rein up as close to the bit as possible and turn him in sharp circles, all the time kicking him with your outside boot to maintain forward momentum. A horse moving forward cannot rear up. Once it seems safe to do so, stop the animal and dismount. Don't panic and jump off a rearing horse, as the sudden shift in balance may pull him right over on top of you.

Emergency Dismount

I hope it never happens that you're forced to dismount from a horse because there's real danger of it flipping over. If, however, dismounting becomes necessary, act quickly. Determine which way is safest to jump and take both feet out of the stirrups. Lean far forward while lifting one leg—the one on the opposite side of the direction you plan to jump—as high as you can. Let go of the reins (this is very important, as you may pull the horse over on top of you if you forget and hold onto them) and, pushing off the horse's neck, leap off the horse as far to the safe side as you possibly can. Try to land on your feet, but if that seems impossible, cover your head with both arms, and roll quickly out of harm's way the instant you hit the ground.

Kicking at Other Horses

If your horse tends to kick at other horses coming up behind, the first thing you must do is mark your horse's tail with a red ribbon or cloth so that other riders are warned to keep a safe distance behind. Then work on retraining. It helps if you have an experienced friend or two with steady mounts who can ride with you. Gradually have them ride their horses closer and closer behind yours while you watch for any signs of aggressive behavior from your horse. As soon as your horse pins back its ears in warning, give a quick snatch on the reins and say "quit!" If he attempts to stop as another horse approaches from behind, kick, bat and/or spur him forward vigorously. If he does lash out, spank him—*hard*—with a riding crop. Do whatever it takes to make the horse understand that kicking and aggressive behavior toward other horses will not be tolerated. Also if you create a bond between yourself and the horse, he'll feel he can trust you to look out for him and won't feel he must aggressively protect himself.

RETRAINING THE SOUR HORSE

This retraining is quite basic and can be accomplished in a couple of days at best, two or three weeks at most. Start by separating your horse from his mates. When you turn the other horses out, keep yours tied safely in his stall. He'll probably get excited, so stick around a while to make sure he doesn't get into trouble. Once he's settled down, but only then, brush him and keep him company. This might not be advisable for a day or two or three, depending on how long it takes him to accept separation. After a couple of days, when he no longer goes wild upon being left inside by himself and seems to enjoy your company, tie him safely somewhere outside where he can see the other horses, for instance,

To retrain a horse that resists your aids, teach him to give his head to pressure. A horse who is supple and conditioned to giving his head and neck finds it difficult to stiffen and resist.

in your riding ring or by the horse trailer. Again, keep him company when he's being good.

Some horses submit to this quickly; others take much longer and need regular separation training. Horses that readily form strong attachments need to be separated regularly. Keeping such an animal inside by himself once or twice a week or turning him out after the other horses are brought in each day will usually prevent him from becoming too herd bound, and save you a lot of trouble in the long run.

When you keep your separated horse company, put the time to good use. After grooming, stand in close to one side, with a solid wall or fence at his other side, and ask him to "give" while intermittently tugging on his lead rope until his neck flexes and his nose touches your stomach. Repeat this exercise to both sides. Practice this several times over a day or two, until the horse willingly gives you his head to a count of five.

Next, using a simple snaffle bridle, tack up. From the ground, ask your horse to give his head, using one rein rather than the lead rope. Once he submits to this on both sides, take him out to an enclosed place, mount up and ask him to flex his head around to your boot. Remember to use a soft give-and-take motion, so the horse can't just set his neck and shoulder muscles against it. A horse must stiffen his neck against your aids to resist. By teaching him to give and flex his neck on command, you are conditioning him to obedience.

Once the horse is flexing easily to both sides, ride him in small circles, first at the walk, then at the trot. Be sure to work him in both directions. Again, you're loosening the horse's body and teaching him to give to your aids. Work him at walk, trot and stop transitions, still in circles. If he's loose enough and in good enough condition, include an occasional lope (canter) transition. Transitional work keeps him attentive.

Once this work is done, and the horse is consistently listening and obeying, you're ready to ride him away from the barn. If he balks, simply ask him to give his head, and turn him in small circles until the conditioned response kicks in. When it does, he'll relax his body and stop resisting; then move on. Repeat the flexing and circling as needed.

This is the most nonviolent way I know to handle a sour horse. Though it takes some time, you'll end up with a willing, well-conditioned riding partner—this is far preferable to having a horse that goes along reluctantly only because he's forced to, but is stiff throughout and mentally resistant.

HEAD-TOSSING

The physical retraining effort described above will often work well for a head tosser, but you may need to add a few extra measures. The head tosser is fearful of the bit, which has caused him pain at some time in the past; he's learned to evade its action by lifting and tossing his head. Such a horse is called a stargazer. The trouble is that *you* could end up seeing stars if his head comes back far enough to hit you.

When working with such a horse, practice the giving, bending and circling exercises as above, but do so with the aid of a running martingale. Adjust the martingale so the rings the reins run through reach the horse's throatlatch. With this arrangement, the horse is rewarded for lowering his head, and there's not so much tension on his lower jaw that he starts to resist the martingale's action.

When riding a head-tosser, keep your hands soft, but despite the temptation to let go of the reins when he violently resists the bridle, never give the horse his head when it's tossed or raised up in the air; this only rewards and reinforces the bad habit. Instead, keep a firm hold on the reins until the horse's head is lowered, then give him some slack. Take up the slack when he raises his head again. Soon he'll discover that the bit doesn't cause him any pain, and that he's more comfortable with his head down than he is when it's raised.

BUCKING

A bucking horse is usually more frightening to watch than difficult to ride. Most horses, if they have any life at all, will kick up their heels on a brisk day, or upon coming out of the barn, or when asked for a lope. The animal may be finished bucking by the time you realize what's happened. Few horses leap and lunge around the way rodeo broncs do.

Bucking is seldom the problem novice riders expect.

If yours does, sell him to the nearest rodeo, as good buckers bring top dollar.

If your horse should buck, especially out of resistance, sit deep in the saddle, keep his head up by using a short, hard snatching motion on the reins and keep him moving forward. A horse has to get his head down before he can buck hard and will not be able to buck at all if he has good forward motion.

If bucking is a persistent problem and you feel you need extra security, bridle your horse over his halter. Then tie a rope from your saddle horn to the halter ring under your horse's jaw, leaving just enough slack for natural head nodding, but not enough that your horse can get his head way down. If he starts humping up, pull up on this "cheater rope," and you'll surely be able to ride out anything he can dish out with so little slack for his head.

SHYING

Horses shy out of self-defense. Their instinctive response to any perceived threat is to jump quickly away and escape. This is true with most animals, the difference being that, when a dog or cow shies at something fearful, there's no danger of a rider being thrown to the ground.

There is a two-point strategy for shy-proofing a horse. I call it giving the horse the D.T.'s, an abbreviation that stands for desensitization and trust. We desensitize the horse to common stimuli that cause shying; then we teach the animal to trust his handler more than he trusts his own instincts. The two go hand in hand.

Let's say a horse shies at water crossings—a common problem. Though we know the water is shallow and harbors no snakes or other dangerous creatures, the horse, with his shallower visual perception, only sees a hole of indeterminate depth and unknown terrors. Asking him to cross that hole is tantamount to asking him to walk off a precipice.

In this situation we teach the horse that there's no inherent danger in water and that, if we ask him to cross a body of water, it is always safe to do so.

There are as many ways to do this as there are horse trainers. One useful trick is to create a water hole right in front of an outdoor feeder, so the horse is forced to walk through water to eat. Another strategy

To minimize shying, expose your horse to frightening stimuli under controlled conditions.

Most horses are quickly desensitized to even the most terrifying bugaboos. Such training also teaches the animal to trust the handler in frightening situations.

185

involves riding through water with a calm babysitter horse going on ahead. If your horse sees the other animal crossing safely—and drawing farther and farther away on the other side—it's likely he'll follow. You may have to get off the horse and lead him through a time or two, so wear rubber riding boots. In any case, after one or two successful crossings, he'll forget his water shyness.

What of the other kind of shying, when the horse suddenly rears and whirls in a panic, or swerves off to one side, or jumps into a ditch or, worse, out in front of traffic? How to handle these situations? Essentially the same way: desensitization and trust.

Plan to expose a horse with a tendency to shy to many different stimuli. Lead or ground drive him through woods, water and fields. Leave large pieces of flapping plastic (a real bugaboo) tied to posts and feeders. When it's time to bring him in for his evening grain, lead him into the barn over the top of a large sheet of plastic. At first, you may need to stand him near the plastic and offer the grain from your hand. Later you can move farther and farther onto the material, and place the grain right on the plastic itself, until he's taken that first bold step. It won't be long until the horse will walk over it on command. Set out posts and old tires, and lead or drive him first around them, then over and through them. Mount up and repeat this work.

Regularly feed and/or tie your horse where he'll be exposed to traffic, then lead or ground drive him on a fairly quiet road. Better yet, if you have access to a quiet, reliable horse that you can teach your horse to pony from, ride the other horse and pony yours—down the trail, along roadsides, near where farm equipment is operating, past livestock of all kinds. If possible, bring your dog along as added stimulus. Now have someone else ride Old Reliable, while you follow on your horse. Soon your horse will stop overreacting to objects and circumstances.

A horse that throws a shoe or needs shoes may shy because of sore feet, or some other discomfort may put the animal on edge. If your horse starts shying uncharacteristically, check out this possibility. Some horses, especially the more bright, alert ones, never completely get over shying. If you own such a horse, be doubly certain to ride with a hard hat, and always stay alert but relaxed in the saddle. Yours might never be the safest, most predictable horse, but it won't be the dullest, most stodgy one, either. If you simply can't relax and enjoy such a horse, then for both your sakes think about selling him and purchasing a more phlegmatic mount.

186

SELLING YOUR HORSE

Not all bad habits can be broken in all animals. Sometimes you'll need to compromise or accept limited success. There may come a time when you simply don't feel safe and comfortable with a certain horse. Or perhaps you feel *too* safe and see your horse as a deadhead who's no fun to ride. Maybe the horse is too easily and strongly attached to other horses, making your dream of long, solitary rides a nightmare. By all means, investigate all your alternatives: Send the horse to a good trainer, take lessons on him, try everything within reason to acclimate yourself to the animal. But if, despite such measures, you still find yourself wishing for something different, then by all means sell the horse and purchase one more to your liking. There are as many good reasons for selling a horse as there are unhappy horse owners.

Often a person buys a horse that is too spirited or strong willed for the owner's level of experience, but the owner refuses to admit this is the case. He or she keeps the horse and rides with pounding heart, sweaty hands and dry mouth—or avoids riding at all. This just isn't necessary.

There are all sorts of horses out there: fat, thin, tall, short, quick, slow, loving, independent, old, young—and everything in between. The even better news is that horses of every type come in a wide range of prices and colors. With so many in the world to choose from, why not own the horse that is most perfectly suited to give you pleasure? Trying to prove you can handle a certain horse, despite regular problems, only ends up making horse ownership a burden rather than the joy it can be. It's not that great for the horse, either.

Horse buying, selling and trading is a unique category of enjoyment. You never know what's to be found just around that next barn door! So don't be afraid to try different things for a while and, if a certain animal isn't working out for you, find him a new owner who loves him for all the same reasons you don't. Then move on to something different and better. You'll be glad you did.

THE NONRIDING
HORSEMAN

*T*here are many ways to experience and enjoy horses without ever riding one. Because of physical limitation, timidity or simple preference, some horse people restrict their horsemanship to nonriding pastimes. Bravo! It's better to enjoy a horse from the ground than never to enjoy one at all.

There are draft horse lovers whose greatest pleasure is in driving their animals or using them to till the soil on a warm spring day. A neighbor of mine raises and trains Belgian draft horses and lends them to Amish families during the farming season. This man comes by his love of horseflesh naturally, as his father has always kept a couple teams of Cobs for driving. It always gives me pleasure to see this older fellow with his pony cart, his spunky little Cobs nodding in unison, their little feet making fast clip-clop noises on the road. Invariably at least one grandchild is sharing the pony cart with him, thus ensuring another generation of horse fanciers.

High-stepping, fancy driving horses and ponies are exciting. The Morgan and Saddlebred fit this category, as does the Hackney pony. People who are intimidated by the large horse may get great pleasure and learn a lot about horses in general by starting out with miniature horses or ponies. Some never switch.

There is a woman in our community who regularly attends a local horse auction where horses are often sold for slaughter, and purchases animals that have had a rough time in life. She brings these animals home, fattens them up, sends them out for training or retraining and then sells them to families who are waiting for an inexpensive, reliable family horse. She boasts far more successes than failures. Still other horse-rescue people work with animal protection services to provide foster care to mistreated horses.

Breeding horses can be both fun and profitable but must not be undertaken lightly. Regardless of how modest or grand his operation, a breeder should carefully determine what sort of animal he wants to produce and become knowledgeable about the history and bloodlines of that breed. Such a person must become a veritable encyclopedia of knowledge about mare and foal care, and sometimes be on call around the clock during the breeding and foaling season. I don't want to encourage anyone to enter this field of horsemanship too lightly. As a rule, backyard breeders produce too many poor quality "throwaway" horses. These animals often have poor conformation, may have bad temperamental quirks and are frequently trained improperly or not at all. If you think you'd like to raise foals, or even one foal, please do so—but do it responsibly.

Ground training is another area of horsemanship the nonriding horse person can enjoy. I once took in a young horse for a friend who raises Appaloosas. This little polka-dotted fellow wasn't mature enough mentally to be put under saddle. He needed some extra handling and ground training. Though I was relatively inexperienced with young horses, I took my time and had a lot of fun working with him. The experience was not only educational for both of us but was nearly as satisfying as trail riding, which has always been my favorite horse-related activity. I discovered that young horses are an absolute delight to work with. You don't have to be a good rider to be able to teach them the basics. All you need is patience, time, a calm attitude, a willingness to learn—and desire.

Many parents catch the highly contagious "horse bug" from their children. Some 4-H and Pony Club mothers are as knowledgeable about horses as any riding horse person, though they've never sat a horse. Many have no desire to ever do so but are content just to be around horses. This is the reason why some folks keep horses as little more than field ornaments.

For some of us, horsemanship is a sort of addiction, but a positive one. To stand at the kitchen door, morning coffee in hand, and watch horses run and dance and play through rays of early morning sunshine is sheer joy. We learn to crave the warm, pungent smell of horse, hay and sweet grain, and no narcotic will ever beat the calming effect of leaning a head into a big, warm friendly side and working away our daily cares with curry comb and dandy brush.

Such are the simple pleasures of the true horsemen.

189

Appendix I

AGEING A HORSE/
CONFORMATION

AGEING A HORSE

Ageing a horse is as much art as it is science, and it takes time to develop this ability. It helps to be familiar with the physical characteristics that help us determine a horse's approximate age.

As a horse ages, its body begins to lose muscle mass. This process usually begins by about age ten, so that a 1,000-pound horse may, by the time it reaches its mid-teens, weigh only 900 pounds, despite good nutrition. A young horse's skin fits tightly over an underlying layer of smooth, well-toned muscle tissue. An older horse's muscles are usually less smooth, perhaps even ropey looking, and the skin and skeletal system both begin to sag. This will usually be most obvious in the back, neck, abdomen and loin areas. The older horse's legs may exhibit signs of wear and tear in the form of lumps, swellings and scars. Also, the area over the aged horse's eyes often becomes hollow. An aged animal's overall look may be rather dispirited when compared to a younger animal.

But all the above changes are relative, and most physical signs of ageing vary from horse to horse. Some horses of twenty maintain their physical vigor, spiritedness and good looks, while other, much younger animals appear aged. The horse's teeth are a more certain guide to a horse's age, especially when considered in conjunction with other physical characteristics.

At birth a foal has four or six temporary molars, two or three to each side of the jaw. Within the first ten months, baby teeth, also called milk teeth, appear. These are temporary incisors; by the time the horse is a yearling, there are six of these small, white, smooth temporary

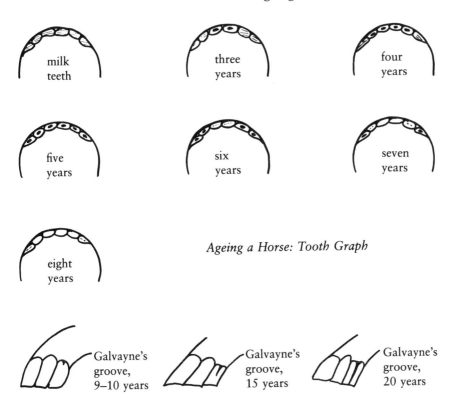

Ageing a Horse: Tooth Graph

incisors on each jaw. At about two and a half the horse sheds its two center milk teeth, which are replaced with permanent teeth. At three and a half four temporary teeth have been replaced. Usually by the time a horse is five years old, all the temporary incisors have been replaced by permanent teeth.

Each permanent tooth has a hollow mark, or cup, in the center. These cups fill with food particles, debris that causes the hollow to darken and turn black. As the horse ages and the teeth are gradually worn down, these dark hollows fade and then disappear. The process begins with the four center incisors and moves outward.

Because the lower incisors are easier to examine when the horse's mouth is opened, the graph included here illustrates typical ageing changes in the horse's lower incisors. Upper incisors lose their cups at a slower rate.

Once the horse reaches the age of eight the cups on the lower incisors are worn away. At age nine or ten a horizontal groove, called

Galvayne's groove, begins to form at the top of the corner incisors. By the time the horse is fifteen years old, the Galvayne's groove runs halfway through the tooth, top to bottom. When the horse is about twenty, the groove runs the length of the tooth. This process then starts to reverse itself so that by the time a horse reaches the age of twenty-five, the groove runs from the center to the bottom of the tooth. Once the groove disappears altogether, the horse is said to be smooth-mouthed, or very aged.

In addition to the changes in the teeth, the horse's jaw changes shape with age. Note in the accompanying graph the difference in the horse's jaw and tooth shape between the ages of nine and twenty. The jaw line and teeth jut more and more outward as the horse ages.

CONFORMATION

There are a number of conformational points that help us determine the strength, agility, riding comfort and durability of a horse. Some conformational faults are more serious than others; an unattractive head, for example, will not limit an animal's use the way a weak back will. Learning to judge conformation takes time, and the different uses we put our animals to require different body types and characteristics. A cutting horse, for instance, must withstand tremendous torsion on all four legs and be able to turn on a dime and stop quickly. Such use requires a rounded, well-muscled croup, good bone, a balanced frame, a well-set head and neck and good legs. A horse used for trail riding, on the other hand, needs to be surefooted, sound of lung and leg and sensible.

Each breed has physical characteristics that differ from other breeds. The croups of Appaloosas are round and heavily muscled, while the ideal Arabian croup is nearly flat; a very high head is desirable on a Morgan but usually less acceptable on a Western-style pleasure Quarter Horse. Because of such conformation variables, the inexperienced horse person would be wise, when considering the merits of a particular horse, to seek the advice of a veterinarian or more experienced horseman.

Overall Balance

When you first observe a horse, look to see if its overall body structure is symmetrical and well balanced. Does the height of the withers closely approximate the height of the horse's croup? Though horses younger

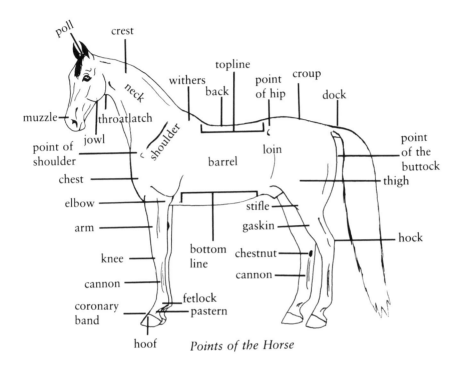

Points of the Horse

than four years often grow first at one end and then the other and therefore look higher in front or back, a mature horse should have a level topline. If not, then the horse will likely have an unbalanced, uncomfortable way of going. Does the horse's topline from withers to hip match the length of the bottom line? The various parts of the horse should fit tightly and smoothly together, each section joining to the next with eye-pleasing angles. This is not just for the sake of aesthetics but because a horse so fitted will be athletic, able to do what you ask and comfortable to ride.

Leg Conformation

Perhaps the most important consideration when evaluating the relative merits of a horse is: How good are its legs? Like a building, a horse is only as good as its foundation.

The accompanying illustrations depict the ideal leg conformation when the horse's legs are viewed from various vantage points, as well as a few common faults. The horse's legs should come close to the ideals pictured here. Dramatic deviations from these ideals weaken the horse's structure. Some conformational faults, such as cow hocks, are not as weakening or damaging as others, such as sprung knees. A horse whose legs, front and/or back are positioned too close together may interfere with itself when moving. When evaluating such an animal, check for sores, lumps or old scars that might indicate such interference. A warning sign of limited usefulness is obvious puffiness in the legs, particularly in the hock, at the back of the cannons and around the fetlock joint and coronary band, especially when combined with legs that are not well formed and straight.

The front legs are of particular importance. A horse carries 60 to 65 percent of his weight on his front end, and difficulties with the front legs account for the majority of soundness problems. To evaluate the front legs, stand back and check from all angles to see if both legs are acceptably straight and similar in construction. When viewed from the front, the upper leg should be well muscled, with straight, clean (not lumpy and bumpy) bone running into the center of the knee. The knee should be large and shaped like a shield, with the flat part facing straight forward. The cannon bone should run straight down from the knee to the fetlock joint, and the fetlock likewise should be clean, strong and well formed. The pastern below the fetlock joint should exhibit no severe inward or outward twisting but should be well squared under the horse's fetlock. Likewise a well-formed, appropriate-sized foot should be centered under the leg. The foot at the top should be larger around than the fetlock joint and flare outward to the bottom.

Pay particular attention to the horse's pastern, side view. The fetlock joint and pasterns serve as shock absorbers and bear a great deal of stress over time. Excessively long, sloping pasterns place extra strain on the ligaments and tendons, often causing soundness problems. Very upright pasterns are equally undesirable, as they do little to soften concussion. Horses with this conformational defect generally have short, choppy gaits and may suffer from ringbone, sidebone or navicular disease. The ideal pastern is moderately long and sloping, the angle of the pastern approximately matching the angle of the hip and shoulder lines.

The back legs should also exhibit good bone and acceptable straightness, "acceptable" being a highly relative term. For some breeds, cow hocks are not only acceptable but desirable. Angulation of the hind leg conformation varies dramatically from breed to breed and discipline to discipline, so that the highly angular construction that is acceptable for a gaited horse would be considered a serious fault in a Quarter Horse

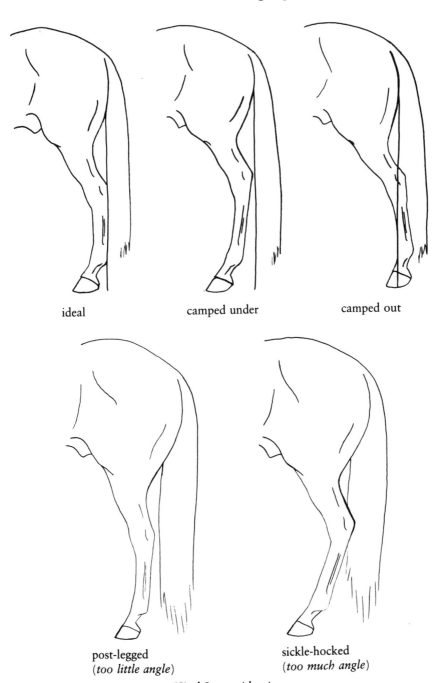

ideal   camped under   camped out

post-legged   sickle-hocked
(*too little angle*)   (*too much angle*)

Hind Legs, side view

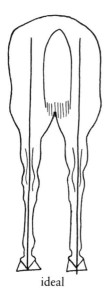

ideal

cow-hocked, toes-out

bowlegged, toes-in

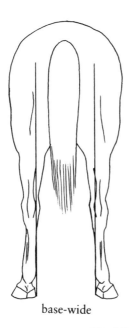

base-wide

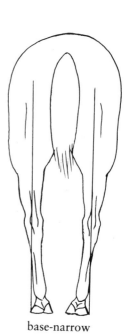

base-narrow

Hind Legs, rear perspective

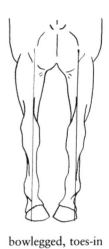

ideal   stands close, toes-out   bowlegged, toes-in

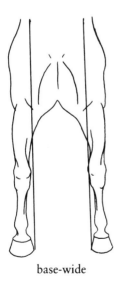
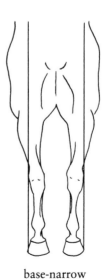

base-wide   base-narrow

Forelegs, front perspective

shown at halter. You want to be assured that the horse's back feet don't interfere with its front feet at any gait, and that the legs aren't conformationally weak because of poor muscling, light bone, too sloping pasterns, very obvious crookedness or a combination of angles that make for an excessively weak conformation. A horse that is out at the hocks, pigeon-toed and camped out in back, for example, would have very little solid foundation squarely underneath itself; as a result, the tendons, ligaments and joints would bear continual stress. Hocks for all types of horses should be large and smooth. Also, because many horses suffer chronic stifle problems, make absolutely certain the stifle joint shows no evidence of locking, swelling or stiffness.

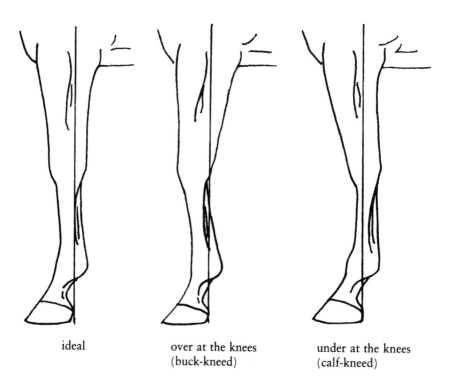

ideal

over at the knees
(buck-kneed)

under at the knees
(calf-kneed)

Forelegs, side view

Head and Neck

Many horses have been unwisely purchased on the merits of a pretty head alone. While it's true that a horse's head tends to reflect its character, such evaluation is by no means foolproof, and a pretty head may be just as easily attached to a weak body as a strong one. It's important to keep any evaluation of the horse's head and neck in perspective, while remembering the animal's intended use; a pretty head and neck are more important assets in a show horse than in a working hunter jumper.

The head and neck of the horse serve to balance the animal's overall movement. For this reason, these parts of the horse should be in proportion to the rest of its body. Ideally the head will have a well-formed jowl; large, dark eyes set well to each side of the head; and a wide, flat forehead. Horses with an exaggerated bump in the middle of the forehead tend to be extremely intelligent and often are troublesome for all but the most experienced, tactful horseman. Horses with a Roman nose (a noticeable bump in the middle of the nose) may be more stubborn than their more refined counterparts.

Ears also reveal a lot about a horse, but this indicator has more to do with the way the horse habitually moves or carries the ears than with their size or the way they are set on the head. A horse that carries his ears flopped out, airplane fashion, is likely to be sour or dispirited. Ears that are habitually pinned back indicate a mean temperament, and a horse that constantly twitches his ears is demonstrating hypersensitivity to his environment and may be rather goosey (or spooky) to ride. Ideally, the ears should be moderately expressive, sized in proportion to the horse, nicely shaped, and set on top of the head just to each side of the poll, neither too close together nor too far down on the side of the horse's head. Horses of some breeds, such as Standardbreds and Tennessee Walking Horses, tend to have large ears that would look downright mulish on a "doll-headed" Quarter Horse but lend an air of nobility to other, usually longer-faced, types of horses.

The horse's nostrils should be good-sized, as this usually corresponds with good lung capacity. Beware of the horse whose nostrils flare with each breath, even at rest, as this may indicate chronic breathing problems.

The throatlatch, where the head meets the neck, should be well defined, but, again, a rough throatlatch may be perfectly acceptable, all other things being equal. Horses with a short weak neck, called a ewe neck, are likely to suffer poor balance and limited endurance and will be uncomfortable to ride. Though the way the horse's neck sets into the shoulder is, again, largely a matter of breed or style preference, the neck should be smoothly set into a well-muscled shoulder at an angle that closely approximates the degree of angulation at the hip and pasterns.

Torso

The horse's body should have good overall muscling, depth and breadth. A very rangy, slab-sided animal often proves to be a harder keeper (has higher caloric needs) than a horse with rounded or bunchy musculature and a short, tight frame. Unless budget considerations are unimportant, do not underestimate the benefits of an easy-keeping horse. Well-sprung, rounded ribs at the barrel and good depth of chest are important considerations, as these indicate good capacity for the heart and lungs. An unusually large barrel, especially when combined with a prominent ridge of muscle running along the bottom edge of the rib cage, may warn of chronic heaves. A heave-y horse's rib cage will widen and the lower abdominal muscles overdevelop in response to the extra effort required for breathing during heaves attacks.

An extremely narrow chest may hint at limited breathing capacity, while a chest that's too wide (barrel chest) will usually result in an uncomfortable and slow ride.

The horse's shoulder should run at a noticeable angle from the point of shoulder up to well-defined withers. A steep shoulder (one that runs too straight up and down) and mutton (rounded) withers guarantee a rough-riding horse, as these defects limit the animal's scope of movement and ability to absorb concussion. Good action generally results from a laid-back shoulder, well-defined withers and a forearm that is longer than the cannon bone.

The horse's back should be level, not roached, with a straight spinal column that demonstrates no outward "lumps" past the withers. A horse with a back that is short from the rear of the withers to the point of hip can handle proportionally more weight than can a longer-backed animal, but an extremely short back may limit suppleness. Regardless of length, the back should be attached smoothly and tightly to the loin and croup areas. Good supporting muscle and connective tissue here are of utmost importance if you want to be assured of having a horse that will not break down under hard use.

Strong abdominal muscles help support the back, enabling the horse to comfortably bear the weight of a rider. The abdomen of a mare that has carried several foals may become somewhat sprung and saggy-looking. Many such brood mares are still suitable for riding, though they should not be counted on for heavy use so long as they are nursing or in foal. A horse that is not a brood mare but that has a saggy abdomen or an abdomen that is longer horizontally than the back generally will not be a very strong, athletic animal. An abdominal line (bottom line) noticeably shorter than the back (top line), especially if combined with long, angular legs, may result in interference, or the horse hitting his front legs with his back feet.

The horse's hindquarters, which provide impulsion, need strength to do the job properly. Strong hindquarters are well muscled and tightly connected to the back. There is good length from the point of hip to the point of the buttock, and the angle at this juncture corresponds to the degree of angulation of the shoulder and pasterns.

Good muscling should continue down through the loins to the thigh and gaskin. This doesn't mean that a horse needs to have the exaggerated, bunchy muscles of the old bulldog type of Quarter Horse; long, flat muscles or smooth, rounded muscles can do the job as well. While a horse with massive, bunchy muscle tissue may exhibit speed over short distances, those impressive muscles require large doses of energy. For this reason, such a conformation is not often found in a horse with great riding endurance.

Limits of Conformation Analysis

While a horse needs to be at least moderately well built to be usable and durable, the best-looking horse in the world is only as good as its temperament, intelligence and training allow it to be. Never allow yourself to be so influenced by a horse's good looks and build that you overlook obvious temperament flaws or serious bad habits. On the other hand, don't be too quick to rule out a willing, kind mount because of some moderate structural imperfections. In the end, it isn't a set of legs and a back that you ride as much as it is the horse's brain and heart.

Appendix II

BREED REGISTRIES

AND HORSE ASSOCIATIONS

BREED REGISTRIES

Here is a sampling of breeds popular in the United States and their registries. Included are several easy-gaited horse breeds. For information about breed associations not given, check the latest *Horse Industry Directory*, published by the American Horse Council, or call or write the American Horse Shows Association (AHSA).

American Morgan Horse Association
P. O. Box 960
Shelburne, VT 05482-0960
(802) 985-4944

The Morgan horse is known for its toughness, durability and style. Morgans are used as carriage and driving horses, park-style show horses and pleasure horses.

American Paint Horse Association
P. O. Box 961023
Fort Worth, TX 76161-0023
(817) 439-3400

The flashy Paint is becoming more and more popular. Breeders of Paints now produce park horses, gaited horses and English-style riding horses, as well as the better-known Western stock type of horse.

American Quarter Horse Association
2701I-40E.; P. O. Box 200
Amarillo, TX 79168
(806) 376-4811

The Quarter Horse is America's most popular breed of riding horse. Versatile and easygoing, this horse often makes an ideal first horse or family mount.

American Saddlebred Horse Association
4093 Iron Works Pike
Lexington, KY 40511
(606) 259-2742

American Saddlebred horses are the Cadillacs of the horse world, representing the epitome of beauty, style and spirit.

Appaloosa Horse Club, Inc.
P. O. Box 8403
Moscow, ID 83843-0903
(208) 882-5578

Tough horses with kind temperaments, this breed, with its many coat patterns, might be called the "designer horse."

Arabian Horse Registry of America, Inc.
12000 Zuni St.
Westminster, CO 80234-2300
(303) 450-4748

Spirited, intelligent and tough, the Arabian horse is valued the world over for these qualities.

The Jockey Club (Thoroughbred)
821 Corporate Dr.
Lexington, KY 40503
(603) 224-2700

Besides racing, Thoroughbreds make excellent event, dressage, jumping and cross-country mounts. Many are also excellent pleasure trail and show animals.

Missouri Fox Trotting Horse Breed Association, Inc.
P. O. Box 1027
Ava, MO 65608-1027
(417) 683-2468

The Fox Trotter boasts a smooth "single-foot" gait that is easy for anyone to ride.

Palomino Horse Breeders of America, Inc.
15253 E. Skelly Dr.
Tulsa, OK 74116-2620
(918) 438-1234

Palominos come in a wide range of beautiful parade colors, from copper to cream to gold to silver, and boast luxurious flaxen manes and tails.

Paso Fino Horse Association, Inc.
100 W. Main
P. O. Box 600
Bowling Green, FL 33834-0600
(813) 375-4331

Paso Finos are horses renowned for their special smooth riding gait, tractability and spirit.

Tennessee Walking Horse Breeders and Exhibitors Association
P. O. Box 286
Lewisburg, TN 37091-0286
(615) 359-1574

Tennessee Walking Horses are long-strided, elegant movers who do a fast "running walk" rather than a trot.

GENERAL HORSE ASSOCIATIONS

Adopt A Horse Program
Department of the Interior
Director, Bureau of Land Management (330)
18th & C Streets, N.W.
Washington, DC 20240

Contact this program for information regarding the adoption of wild horses and burros. It is suggested that anyone contemplating such adoption first read *The Wild Horse: An Adopter's Manual*, published by Howell Book House in 1992.

American Endurance Ride Conference
701 High St., #203
Auburn, CA 95603
(916) 823-2260

Endurance riding is a sport whereby participants race against the clock over a 50- or 100-mile distance. It tests the condition, abilities and stamina of both horse and rider.

American Horse Shows Association, Inc.
220 E. 42nd St., #409
New York, NY 10017-5806
(212) 972-2472

The AHSA is the official sanctioning and rule-making body for horse shows in the United States, and it represents the U.S. horse industry in major international events. Anyone desiring information concerning horse shows, riding programs or the horse industry in general should contact the AHSA office.

North American Trail Ride Conference
P. O. Box 20315
El Cajon, CA 92021-0920
(619) 588-7245

The NATRC is a national sanctioning body for competitive trail rides, holding seventy-five rides per year across the United States. The rides are for any breed of horse, registered or unregistered, and any rider over ten years old.

United States Dressage Federation
P. O. Box 80668
1212 O St.
Lincoln, NE 68501-0668
(402) 474-7632

The aim of the USDF is to promote a high level of accomplishment in dressage in the United States. Dressage is a sport particularly suited to the serious adult rider, and some form of dressage instruction and practice is recommended for any horseman desiring a willing, supple and athletic mount.

United States Pony Clubs, Inc.
893 S. Matlack St., #110
West Chester, PA 19382
(215) 436-0300

This is a horse and pony club for persons 21 years of age or younger. Emphasis is on the English style of riding, but the club embraces all aspects of horsemanship.

RECOMMENDED READING

Most of the books listed below are available through tack shops, general book stores, local libraries or horsemen's catalogs.

The Beginning Dressage Book: A Guide to the Basics for Horse and Rider, by Kathryn Denby Wrightson and Joan Fry. Prentice Hall Press, 1984 (hardcover, 236 pages).

Explains the benefits of dressage training for any type of horse and takes the reader step by step through a dressage program.

Centered Riding, by Sally Swift. Trafalgar Square, 1985 (hardcover, 198 pages).

Uses vivid imagery and sound knowledge of human and equine anatomy to assist riders at every level and in every discipline to achieve a harmonious, well-balanced riding seat.

The Complete Book of Horse Care, by Tom Hawcroft. Howell Book House, 1983 (hardcover, 208 pages).

Just what the title says: a comprehensive guide to looking after the horse. Illustrated with hundreds of color photographs.

The Handbook of Riding Essentials, by François Lemaire de Ruffieu. Harper and Row, 1986 (hardcover, 112 pages).

Describes and illustrates the mechanics, or natural aids, that are essential to good riding. Covers basic to advanced skills.

Horseman's Scrapbook: Helpful Hints for Horsemen, by Randy Steffen. Western Horseman, 1986 (softcover, 143 pages).

An invaluable treasure trove of horse knowledge. Includes money- and time-saving tips that will benefit anyone who owns, rides or uses horses. Profusely and clearly illustrated.

Horsewatching, by Desmond Morris. Crown, 1989 (hardcover, 150 pages).

The question-and-answer format gives interesting and useful general information regarding the horse.

How to Be Your Own Veterinarian (Sometimes): A Do-It-Yourself Guide for the Horseman, by Ruth B. James. Alpine Press, 1985 (softcover, 352 pages).

A superb resource that teaches the reader how to recognize and deal appropriately with all kinds of horse-related health problems. Excellent photographic illustrations.

Schooling of the Horse, Rev. Ed., by John Richard Young. University of Oklahoma Press, 1987 (hardcover, 376 pages).

This book is a classic in its field. It takes the reader step by step through the training of a horse, from foal to finished training. The book is very easy to understand and well written. Besides offering training routines, the author shares many personal anecdotes and colorful information about the history of horse training.

There Are No Problem Horses, Only Problem Riders, by Mary Twelveponies. Houghton Mifflin, 1982 (softcover, 228 pages).

This author's wisdom and experience make her book must reading for trying to cure—or better yet, prevent—a problem with horses.

Think Harmony with Horses, by Ray Hunt. Houghton Mifflin, 1987 (hardcover, 87 pages).

The guru of modern Western horsemanship, Ray Hunt clearly explains his philosophy of human/equine relationships.

True Unity: Willing Communication between Horse and Human, by Tom Dorrance. Panorama West Publishing, 1987 (hardcover, 151 pages).

Tom Dorrance is a popular horseman/lecturer/teacher on the Western riding circuit. His book helps to explain horsemanship, from the horse's point of view.

Index